Full Circle

By
Mady Gerrard

A story of survival and hope

Mady Gerrard
2008

This edition is published by The Duncan Print Group Ltd 2008

ISBN

Duncan Print Group Ltd, Broadwater House, Mundells, Welwyn Garden City, Herts, AL7 1EU UK

printed and bound in England

FORWARD

A Tribute

Having joined the Army in January 1940 and served in Northern Ireland, North Africa, France, Holland, and Belgium after D-Day finally crossing the Rhine into Germany in 1945, I had seen many unpleasant sights. Nothing however had prepared me for the sight which I experienced when I was the first Allied soldier to enter Belsen concentration camp.

A great deal has been written about the prisoners and the conditions in the camp and many others like it which had been established by the Nazi regime. Photographs and personal history give a very vivid account of conditions in these terrible places, but I can assure you that this does in no way compare with the actual experience of seeing with my own eyes the true horror of the situation.

Rather than repeat these facts, they are already covered in the author's own vivid account of the conditions, I would prefer that I give my praise for the fortitude and determination to survive of the many prisoners I have had the honour to meet and talk to.

The attempted annihilation of the Jewish people and the manner of its execution must always remain one of the greatest and most disgraceful crimes in history. The thousands of brilliant and talented people from all aspects of our lives – art – literature – medicine – music – philosophy and every walk of life that was destroyed, is so awful that its magnitude can never be exaggerated.

In spite of these horrors the survivors have a history of extraordinary bravery, a determination to survive and the indomitable spirit to never give up hope. This must be an inspiration to all of us.

For those who were responsible for the atrocities there can be no forgiveness but future generations of Germans must be allowed to live their lives in our modern society. We must all work to try and guarantee that these crimes are not repeated.

My final sobering fear is that these crimes are already happening again and we must all resolve to fight this situation as vigorously as we can.

John Randall. Monday October 16th 2006

CHAPTER ONE

~ Keszthely – A New Beginning ~

It was just before Christmas in 1935. I was five years old. I stood on the railway station in Budapest saying goodbye to my great aunt who had spent a week buying stock for her wool and needlecraft shop. She lived in a little town called Keszthely on the shores of Lake Balaton in central Hungary. Although she was very old in my young eyes – being in her early fifties – I loved her dearly and sobbed at her departure so much that my father pushed me through the train window as it started to move. I was dressed in a navy blue snowsuit and was delighted to be going on holiday.

I didn't know it then but a new life had already begun for me.

I was an only child, my mother was in the early stages of tuberculosis, which eventually caused her death two years later, and my parents were divorced.

I was thrilled by the prospect of the holiday and the train journey, and was enthralled by the scenery as the landscape turned white with freshly falling snow. We chugged through white washed, brick built stations which had low walls with heart shapes cut in them and platforms that were furnished with benches decorated with red hearts where people sat to wait for the old locomotives to pull in during the summer months. Keszthely was approximately 125 kms away and everything was quiet and peaceful except for the bustle of people carrying Christmas trees on and off the train.

We arrived at Keszthely station to find my great uncle Joseph waiting for his wife with a little bunch of flowers pressed to his chest, and although he must have been surprised to see me – shocked even – he never showed it. I was immediately accepted and I was very excited at the prospect of spending the Christmas holiday with Aunt Gisella and Uncle Joseph as the local taxi took us home. Everything was perfect especially when the following morning Aunt Gisi – as I called her – bought me new clothes and somehow, instead of going back to Budapest after the Christmas holiday, I stayed with them.

They were extraordinary people because not only did they take me in but they also looked after an invalid second cousin of mine named Margaret who suffered from some kind of Muscular Dystrophy, and who could only walk with the aid of a walking frame.

I settled very quickly with my great aunt and uncle and fell in love with my aunt's shop, which contained extremely interesting things for a little girl. It stocked wool in millions of wonderful colours, embroidery silks, tapestries, knitting kits, crochet patterns – indeed needle crafts of all descriptions. In the back of the shop there was a huge table with containers full of an exciting blue powder with some very strange bits of what appeared to be greaseproof paper, carefully piled around the place. The papers were perforated with designs, which were used to print patters on linen, cotton and canvas. This process was achieved by spreading the powder over the perforations allowing, the powder to sift through the holes on to the cloth beneath. The paper was then lifted carefully and the powder on the cloth was fixed by spraying it with methylated spirit.

The ladies of the town used these patterns to follow the blue dots and embroider during their leisure hours. The local farmers' wives, however, augmented their income by means of this cottage industry that had arisen and they produced beautifully embroidered articles during the winter months, when they sewed by the light of oil lamps in primitive houses before the luxury and widespread use of electricity. The latter delivered their finished work to the shop and my aunt paid them and everybody was happy because this was an important part of the rural economy. The winter months were therefore productive for the women and they earned extra money that was badly needed to feed many mouths. A woman could rock a baby's cradle with her feet and embroider, knit or crochet simultaneously with her hands whenever she had a chance to sit down.

Aunt Gisella was very much liked in the town and the shop was a meeting place for mothers and daughters who congregated in order to plan their trousseaus, so bedding, towels and table linen were lovingly collected there. All were beautifully hand-embroidered in finely drawn designs of their own choice and were always decorated with the monograms of the brides-to-be. In those days divorce was very rare and putting initials on treasured pieces of linen was quite safe. I only remember one bride whose initials (at least one letter) had to be altered and very carefully re-embroidered with her new last initial because she was getting married to her second husband. She was the only Jewish girl who ever became a beauty queen and she went on to become Miss Hungary. She was beautiful and her name was Liz Simon. My aunt suggested to her mother, who was not really sure that this second marriage would last, that it might be a good idea to use her maiden initials to eliminate any further risks of having to re-work her bottom drawer. I can't remember whether she took the advice or not but it was a good idea!

We had religious classes – 'Sunday School' every Sunday morning in the hall of the synagogue. Our Mr. Ligety taught us. One Sunday he was telling us about Moses receiving the Ten Commandments carved on to two marble tablets. He told us that as he (Moses) was leaving the mountain, a fire started and burned down all the rose bushes – and other – bushes around him. When Mr. Ligety opened it up for any questions we might have, I put up my hand. I asked him to explain to us how was it possible that as everything was in flames, Moses, who was of course wearing a garment, which was like a dress, long and full, yet the fire did not burn it? Mr. Ligety was not happy about my question, and after class I had to stay behind for a few minutes while he wrote a note to my aunt Gisella, which explained what I had done. I had to promise never in my life, to ask any embarrassing questions about religion again. I am sure that this was one of the (many) promises I did not keep!

I felt secure in my new home and I was surrounded by love and life was wonderful for a child. During those summer months I swam in the safe, sparkling blue water of the lake, the skies were always bright and clear, and the sun always shone – or so it seemed to me. During the winter I walked through the large lovely park after school, and bought roasted chestnuts, which I ate after first warming my hands on them in my pockets. I ice-skated with my new friends and was blown around the lake on iceboats as the wind billowed in our sails. How I loved those carefree years.

Most of the families in Keszthely had Austrian *frauleins* to look after the children. They took us to the park and taught us German and were probably the original au pairs.

My aunt's shop was unusual in the sense that it had an array of freshly baked loaves and bread rolls on a counter just as you stepped inside the door. Those were supplied daily by the town's best baker, and my friends, especially Marta, would come to meet me at around 7.25 am every day and would find me waiting outside the shop with a fresh *Kipferl* (a crescent shaped bread roll) in my hand for her. Then together we would go to the synagogue for the children's service that was held between 7.30am and 7.45am; afterwards we would run off to school.

The town was full of good schools. The most famous one was *The Premontrie Boys' Grammar School* and was run by a French religious order, which was situated in the main square of the town, adjoining the main Catholic Church. The priests in this school were highly educated and were qualified to such a degree that the standard of education there was thought to be one of the highest in the country. It was known as a

Gimnasium and boys from non-Catholic backgrounds were also accepted there. The teachers were very much respected in the town and were very conspicuous in their cream outfits with aquamarine sashes.

We all knew that the teachers at the *Premontrie* had their own hobbies. One of them made rugs in his spare time, which were knotted in the same way as oriental rugs; the only difference was that the canvas he used had bigger holes and his pre-cut wool was thicker. This particular priest became a much respected and valued customer of my aunt and he would come to her for his supplies of wool, canvas and tools for knotting. Another priest – Dr. K – was known to collect nails and screws in a big way. His students told us that, when they were summoned to his room, they had to wait outside in the corridor for a long time while he pushed the heavy containers full of his treasures away from the door. Dr. K came into the shop once and saw my aunt serving a customer with some English (*Clark's*) sewing needles, which were delivered in light, polished wooden cigar type boxes fastened with brass clasps. Every box contained thousands of needles that were all sorted into little compartments according to length.

"I really like that box, Aunt Hoffman," said Dr. K to my aunt.

"You may have it when it's empty", she replied. "Then I'll wait" he smiled.

My aunt patiently emptied the contents of the box into another container and handed it to him, otherwise he would have had a very long wait!

The town also had a Carmelite Monastery where monks in brown cassocks and open sandals were seen busying themselves. Their hair was cut around a completely bald patch on the top of their heads!

There was a Girls Convent School, which was run by nuns, an elementary school for girls and another one for boys, as well as a secondary school for girls between the ages of 10 and 14. There were also a number of church schools scattered around the town so that it was well endowed, educationally, for its population of ten thousand. There was also a university for Agricultural Studies.

Let me tell you a little bit more about Keszthely.

The Jewish Congregation of Keszthely was established as far back as 1699. At that time there were only a few 'pioneering' Jews; the first one on record is a butcher. An interesting detail is that in 1730 two Greek and two Jewish merchants lived in Keszthely. At this time the ones who could afford it kept male servants who were also Jewish. The Jews had their own teacher. Already as early as 1730-35 there was a law that a Jew was not allowed to employ a non-Jewish servant.

In those years Jews used names, which were sometimes combinations of Jewish and Hungarian names. However, in 1781, King Joseph II made all Jews take German names.

The first synagogue in Keszthely was built around 1780 by Count George Festetich. A few years later the Jewish congregation purchased the building from the Count.

There were several societies, which played an important part in the life of the community. They helped the poverty stricken people at the time of sickness or accident. They helped poor students into higher education. They made sure that the flame, which is an important part of the synagogue, never went out. A funny detail is that as early as 1863 they formed an association, which was involved exclusively with matching 'girls' and suitable 'boys' for the purpose of marriage. It was in 1810 when Count Festetich first allowed two Jewish families to move into the centre of the town, which actually started the assimilation of Jews with the rest of the people. The number of Jewish people living in Keszthely grew from 260 in 1828 to over 1,000 in 1900. In this little town, they were so keen for good education they had a high school – 'gimnasium' – in 1772. This was supported by the Count, the Town Council and also the Jewish community.

In the year 1850 the tiny Jewish community opened their own school. First they had two classes, later the little school graduated into four classes. In 1870, when the school got to be too big for just one teacher, they gave the school buildings to the 'regular' school, where from then on Jewish children were attending together with all other children.

The boys' 'gimnasium', which was established by Count Festetich, accepted Jewish students. The number of these students grew every year; they were keen students and the school was excellent.

The congregation had its first 'Cantor', a Mr. Goldmark. His son, who was born in 1830, later became (Charles) Karoly Goldmark, a well-known composer.

At this time all Jews in the Empire had to pay a tax, which was called 'tax for patience'. This tax was established by Empress Maria Theresia, who said, "The Jew, because we tolerate him, has to pay for our tolerance". Later Emperor Joseph II kept this up, but changed its name to 'ministerial' tax. This was stopped later on.

There was a big 'popular uprising' in Hungary in 1848. During it there were Jews serving in the forces and they were able to get 'commissions' too.

The list of names from this Uprising in 1848 contains family names, which are the same family names as the list – almost one hundred years later – put together in 1944, so many of those families have lived in Keszthely for a hundred or more years. (But, of course, it was a good place to live in).

In 1848, of 180,000 troops 20,000 were Jewish, which proves that the Hungarian Jews were good citizens, assimilated with 'Hungarians'. In 1867, at last Jews became (officially) citizens with full rights.

Towards the turn of the century, around 1895, a new association was established. Its main project was to help poor girls about to get married.

In 1896, Hungarians celebrated the country's first century. In the synagogue in Keszthely the rabbi conducted a special service saying thanks for their wonderful life in the country. Dr. Alexander (Sandor) Buchler, who was rabbi until 1944, was elected in 1887.

Keszthely produced some famous people, one of them was a Mr. David Schwartz (1850) who made the first 'dirigible', and Zeppelin used his design later on.

By the turn of the century the Jews were well established in Keszthely, which helped the town's finances. They paid big amounts of monies, for example to the Premontrie gimnasium, so that they were able to take on poor students.

When the First World War started in 1914, every able Jew took part in the fighting. Many of them received the highest acclaim, medals, and even the rare 'Maria Theresia' award. Of course, many of them paid the 'ultimate price'. 40% of all war casualties were Jewish. In spite of this, by 1920, the Hungarian Government turned against Jews and declared them 'unreliable'. Slowly things happened; the 'Numerus clausus' came in which made it very difficult for Jewish students to get into universities. (My GP in New York, for example, studied in Padua, Italy, because he could not get into university in Budapest, although his family had been living there for four or five generations).

Hungary had a new 'Minister' from 1921 to 1931. He stopped the raging anti-Semitism and reinstated the equality of Jews. In 1930 they started a new 'Club' in Keszthely. It was a 'Ladies Club' in which Jewish and non-Jewish ladies worked together for Charity. All the money went for the helping of poor people, regardless of religion. Life was good, although the shadow of anti-Semitism was never too far away.

I was already well known to the priests, not only because I had helped in the shop from the age of five, but also because in 1937 there was an Ecumenical Congress in Hungary. This was a very big event for the mainly Catholic town and for months everyone had been planning for the big day when Cardinal Pacelli would arrive to represent Pope Pius XI. The Cardinal was to arrive by train and a suitable committee would meet him at the station. The old red carpet was taken out of moth balls, cleaned and would eventually be rolled out for him, but before this could take place a child had to be chosen to present a bouquet of long stemmed red roses to his Eminence. The town, as I have already stated, was small, but even so it was quite a surprise for my aunt when she was told that I was the child who had been picked for the unparalleled honour of presenting the Cardinal with the red roses. You see my name was Goldgruber, which is a very German-Jewish name. I think they must have known that the Cardinal was not a talkative person and that he was very unlikely to ask me my name!

At any rate, I stood at the railway station, aged seven, looking very smart and wearing a navy double-breasted coat, with my dark brown hair cut in a fashionable 30's style suitable for my age. I had dark brown eyes and a small nose – obviously suitable to represent the little Catholic town, which on that day was the most important place in the whole country. A delegation of VIPs were there too, all very silent and excited. The Cardinal came and stood before me and looked down at me from a great height. I handed over the roses, he thanked me and, my duty done, I resumed my place with my aunt.

In 1998 I took my art student grandson to Rome where we took a conducted tour around the magnificent St. Peter's Basilica. Our tour guide was a beautifully dressed elderly Roman who spoke excellent English with just a trace of an accent. It was a pleasure to listen to him. After showing us around and on the way out to the main entrance he pointed out the grilles on the beautiful marble floor, which covered the graves of the former Popes lying beneath. We came to Pope Pius XII and

I said, "Tell me Signore, am I correct in thinking that Cardinal Pacelli became Pope Pius XII?"

"Why yes, Signora" he replied, "and a very charismatic Pope he was too".

I told him how, when I was a child, I had presented him with the roses.

"Signora", he said "what a remarkable story".

"Signore", I continued, "I haven't told you the punch line yet. I was as Jewish then as I am now, and they chose me from all those Catholic children".

I don't think the Roman gentleman could quite digest the facts but he took me into a corner of the Basilica anyway and showed me a very large statue of my Pope. Charismatic he might have been, but he did nothing to help us or prevent the slaughter of innocents during the Holocaust.

Now, looking back after all these years I feel that I was possibly chosen by some of the people who had used me as a bridesmaid several times in the Catholic churches at Catholic weddings. Obviously we were considered a part of the Christian community in which we lived and consequently this was partly why we felt such a false sense of security in Hungary. We felt that nothing bad could possibly happen to us because at that time there was no discrimination against the Jews.

But back to life in Keszthely.

On the whole, our Jewish congregation was modern and liberal. I remember meeting our Rabbi, Dr. Sandor Buchler, in the delicatessen buying slices of ham, which he must have enjoyed for his tea like all of his followers. Friday nights and Saturday mornings were celebrated with services held in the Synagogue. The High Holidays were very noticeable because the Jewish shops were closed and we did not attend school. During the Yom Kippur service (for the atonement of the dead) people who had not lost relatives could leave the Synagogue and I remember being the only child who stayed to say a prayer because my mother died in 1937.

One of my teachers, Jolan Pflanzer, was asked to explain to me that my mother was dead. She called me into the staff room one day, asked me to sit down, and said "Mady, I have some very sad news for you. You know your mother has been ill for a very long time, don't you?"

She sat quite close and was looking at me, searching for signs to continue.

"Well, I'm afraid your mother has passed away – do you understand what I'm saying, Mady?"

I nodded. She was very kind and gentle with me. It must have been an extremely difficult and unpleasant task for her to perform. After all, how do you tell a seven-year old child that she no longer has a mother?

I was very saddened, but the fact that I had spent two years living happily with Aunt Gisi, who was so full of love, must have made that terrible loss easier to bear. Not having lived with my mother, although I visited her regularly, and the fact that I was too young to fully understand, eased the pain at that stage, but it was to affect me very deeply later on. My new family and friends comforted supported and gathered around me in my tragic loss.

My recollection of my mother was that she was very beautiful. She had very dark, long shiny hair, a lovely face, slim figure and nice hands. She was a smart woman who loved life and loved to look very elegant. I remember her having dozens of pairs of elegant shoes, evening dresses, fur coats and everything a fashionable lady of her time had to have.

One of her evening dresses must have made a great impression upon me. It was made out of black lace; the skirt part made in a number of ruffles and when I saw it I thought it was the most beautiful dress in the world. Unfortunately during one of the balls she went to she drank a very cold drink, it 'burnt' her lungs; she developed tuberculosis, and like all TB sufferers, died. There was no penicillin yet. There was no cure. My beautiful mother, age 31, passed away in a hospital far away from Kispest, where my whole family lived.

They decided to put her to rest in a cemetery, miles away from Kispest, only because my rich relatives wanted to save money. You see it would have been too expensive to transfer her back to Kispest. I have been visiting this very old cemetery for many decades and every time I go there I always stop at the first grave facing the entrance.

The story of that grave is that a very young rabbi had conducted the first service at the official opening of this Cemetery. During the sermon he said that the first person that would be put to rest in this newly opened cemetery would be blessed and special. Unfortunately, as he left the service and was crossing the road, a car knocked him down and he died immediately. Alas, he was the first person to be buried in his cemetery.

I was very fond of Miss Pflanzer. She was a spinster from an upper middle-class family who lived with her sister and brother-in-law in a smart, residential part of Keszthely near the lake. Their house was built in dark brownish brick and it had a number of carved wooden terraces around it. It was large and old and looked like a miniature castle – very different from their neighbours and very grand. Miss Pflanzer had her own apartment in the house where some of us were occasionally invited for afternoon tea. She was a tall, dignified lady who wore her hair swept up on top of her head and was elegant with a beautiful, fragile face. I still remember her smart suits, long skirts and blouses with little ruffles around her neck.

Almost all our teachers were unmarried and we never understood the reason why. Later in high school we had an art teacher, who was pretty and much younger that the rest of them. Suddenly we noticed something going on between her and our physical education teacher – 'something' developed into marriage, which was very unusual amongst the teachers those days.

CHAPTER TWO

~ First Love – Memories & Changes ~

Life carried on and I almost became a native of Keszthely. My friends liked me and I was "one of the crowd". It was during this time that I fell in love with Steve, who was three years' my senior. Yes, it was possible at that early age of seven or eight, and I still feel that Steve was the real love of my life. He had brown curly hair and lovely blue eyes.

I would like to write pages and pages about Steve, but it is very painful. It is also difficult to remember all the details of my "first life", as I sometimes call it. They were the years between seven and fourteen for me, and ten and seventeen for him.

In 1940, Steve, John (Jancsi) – Marta's brother – and Imre, the boy Marta loved at that time, celebrated their *Barmitzva*. The boys were thirteen. It was their big day and they had been carefully prepared for the ceremony by the Rabbi. It took place at our synagogue on the Jewish Sabbath, and they were dressed in their Sunday – or rather Saturday – best, and looked smart and handsome. The *Gimnasium's* velvet caps with the enamelled emblem of their Catholic school were worn proudly on their heads like any of their Christian classmates. The Rabbi blessed the boys after their collective prayers in Hebrew and their individual speeches in Hungarian, and we all felt a definite spiritual presence during the service. We gave them gifts commemorating that day which they would be able to keep for the rest of their lives.

The parents had put a great deal of their hearts into their sons' special celebration day and Steve's parents, like the others, had organised a party for him. The parties were carefully timed so that we could attend them all. I remember Steve being proud of me –"his steady girlfriend". I was only ten, but I was very happy and life was wonderful and we were secure.

Steve had already decided at that time that he wanted to go to Medical school after his graduation from the *Gimnasium*. I was happy about that, because I was sure he would become the same sort of man that Dr. Andrew Rosenberg was – the GP whom we loved dearly. The three boys were surrounded by family, friends and love.

Steve and I spoke many times about our future lives together, when he would become a doctor and I would become an Art Historian – it sounded so wonderful – and still does. Even today I look at my youngest granddaughter and try to compare her with myself in 1944, but it was a different era. We were not streetwise, and certainly not as sophisticated as children are today, but we were more adult in many ways. For example, some time later in 1942, one of Steve's school mates who was two years older than he was and whose name was George Cziffer, came up to me and said "Mady, would you like to go out with me?"

"No thank you", I replied. "I'm very serious about Steve and I could never be unfaithful to him". I was so certain about my feelings, even at that young age.

Steve's father owned a textile store, which was in a shopping centre near the Carmelite Monastery that bordered the town, and led out to the countryside. There the roads were lined with beautiful old chestnut trees, and beneath them horse drawn carts were piled high with fresh farm produce on market days.

The peasants and farmers sold anything they could grow or raise from vegetables, from freshly picked fruit, to live chickens (I hated the idea of killing them), and freshly caught fish. They sold cottage cheese, smoked hams and sausages made on their farms. You could sit in a fish restaurant on the side of the lake and watch the fishermen bring in their catch and choose whatever you wanted to eat straight out of the water. This restaurant was large with tables and chairs placed outside in the summer time. The rooms inside were furnished in a beautiful Hungarian ethnic style and the particular style of this restaurant was called "*Irasos",* meaning "written" embroidery. It was made up of one colour only and looked as though someone had drawn twists and twirls on to hand woven linen. Different districts had different folk-crafts and different designs for their embroidery, and my aunt's shop produced "*Irasos*" tablecloths, curtains and cushion covers that were embroidered in red. It could be red or blue, sometimes green; in this restaurant everything was embroidered with red.

Life was simple then and uncomplicated; there was no television and there weren't too many temptations, either. My aunt and I spent the winter evenings sitting at either side of a table, knitting and reading our books, which were propped up against two identical sweet dishes carved out of soapstone. The radio played music and we enjoyed the peace and tranquillity. Aunt Gisi wore her hair piled in a bun on top of her head and she always kept her spare knitting needles (there were five to a set) stuck in it. She looked just like a porcupine!

At that time, during the late thirties and early forties, the biggest break a girl from our small town could have was to meet and marry a boy from a big town; to meet and marry a man from Budapest was considered unbelievably fantastic luck. Today it would be like a country girl marrying the President of the USA.

Let me tell you about such a girl whose name was Irma Kertesz. (The same name was translated to 'Curtis' by the world-famous movie star, Tony Curtis, whose mother's maiden name was Kertesz). Translated, the name means 'gardener'.

Irma was the daughter of a little Jewish tailor who must have made lots of money because, suddenly Irma, her sister Ella and their mother all appeared in the synagogue one morning dressed in brand new black Persian lamb coats. At that time no fashionable Jewish princess would wear Persian lamb in other than black. However, so that we all understood that they were custom made for them alone; they were all cut in different styles. People started to talk, in and out of the Synagogue, and started to wonder what the future husbands of the two girls would be able to give them if their father spoiled them with such gifts.

Irma soon found and married her "Prince" from Budapest, and a few months later honoured her parents with a visit. Irma, having been born and bred in Keszthely, announced condescendingly to her family and former friends, "I don't know how people can live in a place where you can't even buy smoked salmon!" (There were ten thousand people living there, some were rich and some were poor, but we all managed to live without smoked salmon!)

In summer, large groups of children would walk the 5 kilometres from Keszthely to the now world-renowned Spa at Heviz. The lake at Heviz is very warm all year round because hot springs containing health-giving minerals pours into it. Beautiful water lilies float on its surface, people swim slowly amongst the flowers and benefit from this natural source of healing. In the winter, the steam given off from the water eases painful joints and muscles and after swimming, massages are available at the luxury hotels. One can stay in the blissful surroundings and breathe in the soothing atmosphere.

In the old days many members of the European Royal families, aristocrats and movie stars, went to Heviz to benefit from its treatments. The lake is situated amidst beautiful parks, and the smell of millions of semi-tropical flowers growing wild wafts through the air.

One of the aristocrats – Prince George Festetich – a member of the Hungarian Royal family was a local legend. He was very, very rich and lived in his 365-roomed palace in Keszthely. The interior of the palace was covered with exquisite hand-made tapestries depicting magnificent hunting scenes or other elegant patterns. The rooms were filled with hand-carved furniture made by master craftsmen, the floors were covered with the most beautiful oriental rugs and the walls were hung with valuable portraits of his ancestors and the Hungarian Royal family. The Prince was in his late thirties when he decided to marry and chose a beautiful lady who, I think, was a member of an Austrian aristocratic family and she was immediately adored by the town's folk – they had found someone to worship at last. The Princess soon gave birth to a little boy, a lovely child with blonde curly hair. She started to order things from our shop such as hand knitted bed jackets in very fine wool worked in light pastel shades with huge pom-poms on twisted cords that held the two sides together. I was commissioned to make those pom-poms and was actually paid for doing them. That was the first money that I ever earned.

I have to mention here that we made lots of those bed jackets for the Princess because she presented them as gifts to several other princesses and even queens around Europe. The only name I remember was Elizabeth, who became Britain's Queen Mother. I often wonder whether she enjoyed wearing one of them. Maybe she did a few years later during the war when the palace was not very warm.

The young Prince was often brought to the shop, in a small, handsome, pony-drawn carriage, by his nanny who would place him on the counter. 'Aunt Hoffman', (everyone called my aunt that) would measure or fit him for a crocheted jacket, a hat or whatever we were making for him at that time.

Towards the end of 1938 the adults were getting nervous; they were terrified of the consequences of a war, which seemed certain to break out in the neighbouring European countries. Hitler had been in power since 1933. The *Anschluss* (the Union of Austria with Germany) took place on 12 March 1938 – *Kristallnacht* (the night of 'the broken glass' when the *Nazi Sturm Abteilung* in Germany and Austria mounted a concerted attack on the Jews, their synagogues and their property) soon followed in November of the same year. Clever Jews – rich Jews - were leaving for America or England.

My father remarried around that time. His new wife called Manci (Margaret) was also Jewish. She had never married previously and lived in a flat in Keszthely with her mother. This she continued to do after the marriage. My father always did his best to visit me on his weekend breaks and from that time visited both of us during his limited free time.

He was an attractive, lovely man with good taste and grand ideas. He was in the timber business, but never successful. He always looked very elegant though and had very posh friends. These friends did not come from the same background as my father did; in other words they were not Jewish; at least, many of them were not. Some of these friends even belonged to Hungarian aristocratic families, although not to the very famous ones. 'Hanging out' with people in the higher classes. They did things Jews never did. For instance they called out each other for duels.

I have to remind people that this was the early '30's, when every self-respecting nobleman, aristocrat or just ordinary middle-class man (young, university-age men) wanted to be educated in Heidelberg, Germany. I don't know the reason, but I do know that having a scar on your face, which you picked up during a duel, was all the rage! Without one you were not totally accepted in the 'right circles'. Well, my dear Father – long before he got married – was called for one of these duels, although not in Heidelberg, but in Budapest. I think he had a misunderstanding – discussion with a young nobleman and a minute later he was 'called out'. Luckily for him, a more mature man appeared and sorted things out. Not knowing anything about fencing, I might not have had the chance to be born some years later. – I feel very sad at not being able to spend longer with him than the spring of 1944.

Something happened which made a big difference to our lives at that time. My Great Uncle Joseph, who for years had suffered from Diabetes and who had needed daily insulin injections, passed away. It turned out to be a lucky break for him in that it saved him from being deported and gassed a few years later.

One day during 1940 I was asked to go into the parlour where my aunt was having tea with two ladies. They were the sisters of the local bishop and since neither of them had been married, and neither of them had any children, they had come to offer to adopt me.

They also explained to me, in the nicest possible way, that bad things might happen to the Jews in the future, and that they would like to save me from any suffering. I remember one of them taking a small box out of her handbag, opening it and showing me a pair of beautiful earrings, with three graduated diamonds in each. This would have been my christening present, I was told. The proposal was something that I should have thought over very carefully but I was too young and not knowledgeable enough at that stage to realise what it could have meant for me. I said, after a few minutes, that I couldn't leave my friends, but I thanked them for their very generous offer. Thinking back after all these years, the late Mrs. Eleanor Roosevelt, who was married to Mr. Franklin D. Roosevelt – the American President between 1933 and 1945 – comes into my mind. She is reputed to have said:

"Whenever I am in a dilemma, my head says one thing and my heart says the opposite, I try to follow my heart because even if I am wrong I feel good about it!"

Well, I certainly made the wrong decision that day, and I feel sad that I never had the chance to thank the kind spinsters for their offer, because when I returned in 1946 they had moved and I never saw them again.

At that time, Hungary was still feudal and was owned and ruled by just a few rich families. My stepmother Manci's sister Sarah was married to a lovely man who was the manager of a very large estate belonging to one of the richest aristocratic families in the area, and so during our Christmas holidays all the children related to her were invited to stay with them. We were picked up from the nearby railway station by a horse-drawn sledge, similar to the ones used in the film 'Dr. Zhivago', and taken to the estate. It was magical.

At the railway station I met up with Cousin John (Jancsi) who came from Budapest, which was in the opposite direction. Janci was the son of the only brother my stepmother and Aunt Sarah had. He was six years older than I was, and tall and handsome. He used to spend the summer holidays in Keszthely with his relatives. I remember him taking me across the street to buy ice cream in Mr. Popovits's shop.

Their home was not very far away and everything was covered with snow and it was winter wonderland at its best. The outhouses had been filled with pheasants, rabbits, venison and hams, in preparation for Christmas and Aunt Sarah and her maid had been cooking and baking for days. A huge Christmas tree had been brought into the biggest room in the house and, when Christmas Eve came, it was just like Christmas Eve in any Christian home. The candles were lighted and the festivities started. We never even realised that this activity was unusual for Jewish families and we behaved just like other Hungarian families did at Christmas. We were just the same as everyone else, or so we thought.

CHAPTER THREE

~ 1940's – The beginning of the end ~

It was 1942 and the war was in full swing. The Germans and the Axis Powers were masters of most of Europe. They had conquered vast areas of the eastern front and the German armies were laying siege to Stalingrad. We were frightened – really frightened. The adults listened to the voice of the BBC every night in secret behind darkened windows, terrified that someone would hear them. We had soon come to realise that the Hungarians were as cruel as the Germans and were ready to report anybody for any such infringement. Christmas 1942 came and went and the only difference was that Jewish men were conscripted and forced to work in labour camps and sent to far away places like the Ukraine and other parts of Russia. Some were sent to battlefronts elsewhere to serve mostly the fighting troops of Hungary – the real Hungarian soldiers. By this time Jews were not trusted enough to be called up as members of the Hungarian forces. My father and uncles were out there somewhere and we didn't know what had happened to them.

Still, the older Jews could not believe that the head of the Hungarian state, Admiral Horthy, would allow us to be hurt because it was rumoured that his wife was partly Jewish. We didn't know then that Eichmann's last coup was to be the extermination of the Hungarian Jews and that Admiral Horthy would assent to his demands to hand over to the SS the country's 800,000 Jews for 'relocation' in the eastern territories.

During these years we were asked in school to collect any items of clothing for the families of the servicemen on the fronts. I remember pulling out the drawers of the old chest, where my clothes, underwear and stockings were kept. I must have taken this request very much to heart, because the next day my poor aunt could not give me my usual clean clothes, because there were none. I had packed every item of underwear and woollens and taken it all into school for those needy children. – We were all knitting for the soldiers as well. I (very proudly) could make everything the grown women could, thanks to my training in the shop. We knitted balaclavas, knee warmers, mittens and other complicated items, while the younger girls (those without 'my knowledge' of the first craft I have ever mastered) and women who did not really know about knitting made scarves. Every gram of wool was used up; everybody who had anything to 'unravel' did that. We 'skeined' the used wool, washed it, dyed it and re-knitted it. We called it being practical, also desperate. Today we would call it 're-cycling'. I think the 'mother' of the 'refugee blankets', as we know them since the war, was made by us in those sad times.

At the beginning, maybe even the Jews, who were in work camps, received some of the woollen bits we so diligently knitted and sent. They were all in places where the winters were bitterly cold. Warm clothing, in some cases, was saving lives, or at least limbs. The 'workers' of these camps were housed in out-houses, stables and sheds, and the only way they saved themselves from freezing was to keep very close to each other.

They were also very depressed and only their Hungarian Jewish sense of humour cheered them up now and again. I always remember a story my uncle told us. His best friend was a Mr. Swartz, who was very good-looking. (Mr. Swartz's first name was Zoltan, shortened to Zoli). He – Zoli – was going to marry Ili (Ilona) after he returned from Budapest, because Ili and her mother helped him to hide from the Nazis at some point. The story goes: When they really got very depressed in the horribly cold shed, freezing, hungry and very tired from the hard labour, my uncle would ask Zoli to take out Ili's photo, which, after making the usual round amongst them all, cheered them up; they all had a little giggle, because she was so funny-looking!

My uncle would say: "Zoli, are you really going to marry this ugly woman?" The answer was "Yes, I am".

My uncle would then say: "She has no money at all, does she?" Zoli would reply, "No, none".

My uncle continued: "Listen; even if she had 20,000 florints, say you will live together for 30 years that per day is only a few 'fillers'. If someone asked you to look at an ugly woman for a few 'fillers' a day, would you?"

I don't have to tell you that the first thing Zoli did was to tell his wife-to-be what his best friend, my uncle, had said to him about her. He then married her!

Somehow they all survived and returned home. This was the year 1940 or 1941.

One day my aunt and I were in the shop (it was routine for me to help her out after school each day), when one of her best customers, whom she considered almost a friend, came in. This woman's husband owned the largest paint shop in the town and they knew everybody and everything.

"I have great news for you" she said to my tiny sixty-two- year-old aunt. "All Jews are going to be taken away and no one knows where to or for how long".

My frail old aunt must have looked horror stricken. "Of course the *special* ones that everybody likes – like you, Aunt Hoffman – are going to be left alone".

Alas, they were not left alone. The Hungarian slogan in those days was that they all hated Jews, but that they all had a *special* Jew. We will never know if anything would have been different had they all looked after their own *special* Jew.

However, in the spring of 1943 we still tried to have as normal a life as possible, although bad things were happening around us. Our GP, Dr. Andrew Rosenberg, was called up for special duty and we never saw him again. At this time Polish refugees came to Hungary and to our little town and melted into the Hungarian society. We listened to their terrible stories about the treatment that they had received at the hands of the Germans, but we didn't heed the warnings. These were not Jews, but they told us how the Polish Jews were being deported to places with names we had never heard of before – places called Auschwitz, Buchenwald, Ravensbruck, Bergen-Belsen – but we still could not believe that it would happen to us. We still believed that we would be safe in Hungary.

I was one of thirteen Jewish girls in my class. At the age of thirteen the boys were bar mitzvahed, but we were to be confirmed. We didn't realise that confirmation was a Christian tradition. Jewish girls should have been Barmitzvahed. Anyway, the Rabbi and our Religious Instructor, a Mr. Ligeti, painstakingly prepared us for the big day, which was to be held on a Saturday morning, during the normal service in the synagogue. It took weeks of instruction and preparation but thirteen girls of the same age were ready by the appointed day and we stood there in a full synagogue. It was unusual for so many girls to be confirmed at the same time in such a small town. I remember Marta's family presented all thirteen of us with a delicate, hand carved little ivory rose-pin that some poor elephant had donated. Nobody cared about animal welfare in those days and we learned that they didn't care too much about people, either.

Steve gave me an exquisite *Eusin* porcelain statue of a child bending over a beetle with large antennae: the porcelain looked like glass lustre and was made in strong greens, fuchsias and blues. The style was very popular at that time in Hungary and even at that age I had already developed a passion for beauty and colour. By some strange miracle that precious piece of porcelain was restored to me on my return to Hungary after the war and I still have it.

1943 was to be the year of our last family Christmas ever, but luckily we didn't know it at the time. We went to the country to Aunt Sarah and her family as before to play in the snow and to eat the wonderful food she provided. If she'd known that it was to be the last time we'd have the great pleasure of being together and of seeing each other, she would have given us her heart. Only two people survived from that gathering – my cousin John (Jancsi), and me. Aunt Sarah's husband, who was a big strong man and who looked indestructible, died, and no one knows where. Aunt Sarah was obviously gassed on arrival at Auschwitz because she had her young daughter with her. Mothers with young children lasted minutes only. Although the family lived on a large estate in an isolated situation, miles from any other Jews, they were hounded and trawled into the net by the meticulous Hungarian machinery and the thorough scrutiny of the SS that were involved with the Final Solution.

It was also in 1943 that our Maths teacher became ill. She had to have an operation on her face and stayed in hospital. There were no 'supply teachers' left, because all the male teachers were fighting for our glorious country. I was called into the staff room and was told that I would have to teach the form one year below us maths. This was a fantastic honour; I, of course, was very proud of myself and filled in for 2 – 3 months.

I don't remember much about 1944 before the fatal Sunday of 19 March. It was the day when many Hungarian Nazis, as well as ordinary citizens, hung their best oriental rugs over the balconies to greet the German army which was to occupy Hungary until it was driven out by the Russians. Candles were burning in the windows and flowers were being thrown onto the soldiers as they marched through our little country. We knew that it was going to be very bad for us, but being optimistic until the last minute, the adult Jews were still hoping for miracles. For me, that day had a special meaning, because we were going to celebrate Steve's seventeenth birthday. And it was the day that he explained to me that, whatever happens, and wherever we both ended up; when the war ended we would look for each other. We promised to put an advertisement in a certain Hungarian newspaper to find each other. But, alas, I never had the chance to advertise for him.

A number of people committed suicide a few days after the German occupation. Dr. Simon, an eye specialist (the father of beautiful Liz Simon, former Hungarian beauty queen) and Mrs. Simon killed themselves rather than become victims of the Nazis. So did several others. I have been wondering for years if they were right?

After 19 March 1944, we started on the cruelest, most humiliating road the Germans ever designed for us. We were forced to wear the *Yellow Star of David* and because I was clever with my hands I made lots of them for my family and friends. It was a dreadful task for a fourteen-year old girl to perform. We continued attending school and in fact, finished the year. I had an excellent school report and for my end-of-year award, I received a beautiful book called *Miniatures from the East.* I remember it was beautifully produced, with glossy plates printed in brilliant colours. I took this book with me to Auschwitz.

We were forced then to relinquish all our valuables; first our jewellery went, then our silverware – cutlery, coffee and tea sets, and our large fruit bowls, and almost everything else we possessed. Lastly we were forced to give up our homes. After our homes were confiscated we had to live in the ghetto, which was organised for us, in and around the grounds of the synagogue. The little houses surrounding the synagogue were full of people who found it very difficult to live in such close proximity with one another, whether they were friends or relatives. Being friendly with people or even being fond of them was one thing, but being squashed four or six people into rooms, which normally would have accommodated one or two people, was something completely different.

One of the many sad things I had to do was to leave my 13 – 14 dolls behind. They were all sitting on my aunt's beautiful dark green rocking chair. Leaving them behind broke my heart.

By this time I was quite good at knitting, crocheting, and even knew how to sew a little. My dolls were my 'models'. I had dressed them in very nice, fashionable outfits, all made by me. Sometimes I was told to take them into school to show them to our 'Craft' teacher. These I had also loved and have had to leave behind like so many other beloved parts of 'my world'.

In my terrible misery later in the camps I often wondered what happened to my beautiful dolls. Who is playing with them now? Does the girl who owns them know that there was somebody, who also loved them, dressed them, looked after them and had to leave them behind, because she belonged to the wrong religion?

One of my closest friends, Steve's cousin Susie, had a terrible accident whilst living in the ghetto. She was trying to help her mother in the part of the kitchen that had been allocated to them when she accidentally spilled a saucepan of boiling milk over her chest and stomach. The doctor came and her burns were treated, but when the skin healed it was too tight for her little body, and they had to cut most of it off to allow it to heal again. Susie nearly died with the horrendous pain she suffered.

We were in the ghetto for a few weeks and were only allowed out of it at certain times during the day. We were not allowed into public places any longer, but one day I walked through the town in order to say goodbye to my favourite teacher, Gabrielle Kovesi, who taught us Hungarian and History. I took her flowers.

"I've come to say goodbye, and to thank you for all your help over the years" I said quietly.

"I'm not going to say goodbye – I'll see you again, Mady". She looked me straight in the eye as she said those words, and I never forgot them.

During the last few months of our normal existence, I started to crochet skullcaps with a long cord hanging out of the top, which ended in a hand made tassel. This was big fashion and the local milliner got me orders for these caps. I crocheted them, spent hours in the quiet evenings, producing them in all the required colours. They had paid me every so often, but as our lives, as we knew it, came to a halt, they didn't bother to give me the money they owed me. I remember feeling very sad, being 14 years old; not only losing everything else, but also even having to leave behind the little money I had worked so hard for.

Years later, when I returned and asked for the money, they "did not remember owing it to me". It did hurt that they did not feel obligated to pay me, knowing what I had gone through. Is that human nature? I was too young to understand.

CHAPTER FOUR

~ Journey into Hell – Auschwitz & Guben ~

It must have been in the month of June when we were taken out of the ghetto to the railway station in Keszthely.

The townspeople were standing looking at the scene. We must have been over a thousand people, including the surrounding villages, who were rounded up to go with us. The spectators and the prisoners (for that's what we had become), looked similar. They spoke the same language, their bodily functions were the same and they had all lived in the same area for years - for generations in many cases.

Anyone who was not aware of the circumstances would have thought that the people who were being trucked away were identical to those who were staying. Alas, circumstances had changed and suddenly we were being driven like cattle and, like cattle, were being herded into trucks and taken away out of sight to be slaughtered. The onlookers didn't care about our destination or whether we would ever return. Almost all of them rejoiced in the excitement of seeing the mass exodus. The only creatures that were sad were the dogs that we, the Jewish people, had owned. The poor faithful dogs were running after the train, whimpering, barking, crying and howling at our departure. Some of them even tried to jump on to the train, and died in the attempt, and others were shot. We didn't know what happened to the remaining dogs, but we were quite sure that they would be severely punished for showing such devotion to Jews.

We were taken to a town called Zalaegerszeg, which was a journey of about three hours from Keszthely. We were kept there in some buildings for a few days and then we were moved to a huge quarry where we lived in tents. There were some old pre-fabricated units in the quarry, which, in better days, had been used as offices, but they were to serve a different purpose during our stay.

The Hungarian Nazis, called the *Nyilas Party,* held their interrogations in these units and we all knew what was going on when we heard the screams that often emanated from them. I was just fourteen years old, small, ordinary-looking with sad, dark eyes, when one day I was ushered into the offices for questioning.

The Hungarians wanted me to tell them where my family treasures had been hidden. I kept on saying that whatever we had owned had already been taken. (I remembered my tears falling on the baskets of silver that I had taken to the Town Hall and the shock I received at seeing people, whom I knew quite well, greedily taking what we, the Jews, had been forced to forfeit.)

My interrogators didn't believe me and made me remove my shoes and kneel barefoot on a wooden chair – they always started interrogating by hitting the soles of the feet before proceeding to the rest of the body. I was petrified. I tasted terror as I sensed the total helplessness of my situation. Then, just as one of them picked up his whip to start hitting me, the door opened and, miraculously, a Rabbi called Dr. Solomon Halper came in and said something to the man, who immediately dropped his whip and let me go.

I had met Dr. Halper once before on his wedding day in Keszthely. He was an extremely good-looking man and had married the daughter of our Religious teacher, Mr. Ligeti. On his wedding day, he had worn a dark suit with a light blue shirt, which his mother-in-law-to-be noticed – she obviously thought he should have worn a white a shirt. It seems strange that we worried about such details then and stranger still that I should remember such things now.

Unfortunately, I never had the chance to thank Dr. Halper, my Messiah, nor did I ever learn what words he had used to dissuade my interrogator from beating me, because he did not return from his internment.

In Zalaegerszeg, Aunt Gisella, who was sixty-three years old by that time, was kept some distance away from us and was desperately trying to look after my handicapped cousin on her own. She felt very lonely and obviously frightened. My stepmother, Manci, along with her two sisters and their families and I were all together. There was nothing much to do in Zalaegerszeg but play dominoes or read whatever books we had taken with us. I saw Steve delivering food with a horse and cart, but had no actual contact with him. We had no contact with the rest of the Jews from Keszthely, because they were kept in another part of the town, and Steve and his parents were there.

On, I believe, 4 July, the following announcement was made:

"You are all to be taken to a work camp. You are permitted to take only one piece of luggage with you."

Soon lorries came to transport us to the town station where crowds of local people, once again, gathered to witness our departure. They must have known what lay ahead of us, but cheered at our deportation just the same.

Auschwitz

I made my first journey to a foreign land in July 1944, and that first foreign country turned out to be Poland. On 8 July I arrived at Auschwitz after travelling for four days under horrendous circumstances. We were pushed, kicked, and packed in like sardines – forty or fifty people – into the wagons by Germans and Hungarians in uniform. Even the elderly and maimed were shown no mercy. We were padlocked into the trucks that had barbed wired fixed across the high open windows. Some people managed to sit on suitcases or bags; others had to stand for the duration of the journey. Men, women and children; we were given tall tin buckets to use as toilets. This was my first taste of being deprived of privacy. The wagons were opened only a few times during the long journey when we were let out to relieve ourselves in front of everybody. We were given very little food and water, and no means of washing ourselves or keeping clean. We were filthy after being kept in such inhumane and undignified conditions. The manner in which we had travelled so adversely affected the old folk that several of them died in our wagon and their bodies had to be removed by the rest of us. It was the cruellest journey imaginable.

I stood most of the time in the corner of the wagon looking out from the high small barbed windows. When she had the chance, Manci whispered to me:

"Your father and I buried some of our valuables in a garden in Keszthely, and I must tell you where to find them in case we don't get back home."

She was very serious and I was very alarmed.

"Don't be silly", I hissed. "We'll both get back and find them together".

Two of Manci's sisters lived with their families in Keszthely, and the treasure could have been buried in either one of their gardens, or neither. Alas, we did not return home together and I heard later from some woman that Manci survived only a few months, and I don't know where she died or when exactly. I don't need to tell you that I didn't find any buried treasure on my return to Hungary, but I'm sure there are troves of buried silver and gold, and even diamonds hidden all over the country awaiting their owners' return. The Hungarians, who, even if they knew whom it belonged to, would not have made any effort to give it back, must have found most of it.

I don't even have a photograph of my beloved Aunt Gisella who, during the nine years that I lived with her, gave me everything that was good and loving in the most unselfish manner – my own parents could not have given more. Neither do I have a picture of Manci nor any other member of her family who were so kind to me – especially Aunt Sarah and her husband.

We arrived at Auschwitz station early one morning. We were all terrified, not knowing what to expect, and then the Germans opened the wagon doors. The SS guards stood around with their dogs straining at the leash as thousands of helpless, hopeless Jews spewed out to the shouts and orders and kicks of their captors. The noise was tremendous: people were shouting and screaming and the beast-like guards were barking their orders and the dogs were snarling at us. There were Germans strutting about and strange-looking people dressed in striped pyjama-like garments with yellow stars stuck on their backs were rushing around like ants.

Those striped creatures soon told us that some of us would die immediately and some later. The entire luggage we had brought with us had to be piled up as we were rushed off the trains – we were told we would have them back later. In that pile were my school reports and my beautiful book *Miniatures from the East* of which I was so proud. A few couples who had journeyed with us and who had saved their bits of chocolate for a rainy day were forced to put those luxuries on to the piles too. The 'rainy day' did not come, a very rainy year followed, but they did not live to eat the chocolate.

Auschwitz was like a ghost town with the infamous words engraved above its gates announcing ***ARBEIT MACHT FREI – "WORK MAKES FREE"*** – words that will be carved in my mind forever.

On the station we saw a table and two chairs set apart. A tall fair man in uniform stood there. We soon discovered that his name was Dr. Mengele. He was surrounded by dozens of SS guards with their big ferocious dogs and we were surrounded too. Then we were paraded in front of Mengele and, with a gesture of his hand, he indicated whether we should take the right hand queue or the left, which meant nothing to him, but life or death for us. One line filled up quickly with the elderly, with mothers who had young children and with the handicapped and infirm, and it led immediately to the gas chambers. That line contained my dear, kind Aunt Gisella and my sick cousin Margaret.

People were screaming all around us as we were ordered to follow our allotted lines. We were pushed and prodded into ugly, stark rooms and told to strip. We stood there naked and embarrassed and very frightened, and then the primitive showers were turned on and it was our good luck that water gushed out and not gas – so we survived. Our clothes had disappeared – we had no underwear but were given a pair of shoes, which if we were lucky, almost fitted. The sexes had been segregated by this time and we were given a dress each. We were then shoved on to seats and our heads were shorn. I felt the warmth of my hair fall on to my bare shoulders, and on to my naked body. All our body hair was removed giving us the feeling of absolute nakedness. We were then told to put on our dresses – mine was three times too large for me. It was pink and blue and almost touched the ground. We were not given the striped uniforms so often seen in photographs and films because we were not going to be there long. After the initiation we were marched into the open yard and we stood there with no hair, and then the fear really started, and it got stronger and stronger.

A few minutes later a group of men were pushed on to the piece of concrete that we had vacated – our men, fathers, brothers, and in my case the love of my life – Steve. Steve and I had loved each other tenderly for many years, and then when he was seventeen and I was fourteen, we saw each other for the last time and I was bald. It still hurts to think that that was his last picture of me. I stood there only lightly clothed and I felt embarrassed and very, very desperate. He still had on his own clothes and his hair, and that is how I always remember him. It took me forever to get over his loss and I still ask, "What did he do to deserve to be starved to death at age 18 years?"

Every night open lorries filled with thousands of innocent, tragic victims were driven to the gas chambers. Some were screaming, some were crying, but the lorries rolled on as part of the well-oiled death-machine of the Third Reich. Gassing people only took minutes. Sometimes we wondered how the dead bodies were removed to the crematoria and then we started to hear about the *Sondercommandos* who were the special groups of men whose job was to remove the bodies. Sometimes those poor men found their own mothers, fathers, wives, sisters, brothers, or perhaps, most upsetting of all, their own children amongst the dead. This horror cannot be imagined by normal human beings – one had to be there.

The *Sondercommandos* were selected exclusively from professional people. They were mostly Jews, but sometimes a tragic Catholic priest could be found in their midst. They consisted of all kinds of educated people – doctors, solicitors, chemists, archaeologists, etc. The Germans were real perfectionists and needed highly qualified groups of intellectuals to transfer dead bodies from the gas chambers into the furnaces. It may have been yet another means of humiliation for the Jews, but whoever they used for cleaning up the mess that mass murder leaves in its wake, Auschwitz was well organised and no bodies were left around. Auschwitz was clean and tidy: we didn't even have lice.

My husband's late brother, Peter was a highly qualified surgeon in Hungary. When he was only seventeen years old, they took one of his kidneys out. He was living – existing in Auschwitz with one kidney, although it was very difficult even for the majority, who had two.

Peter, because he was a doctor, was 'selected' to be a member of the very exclusive Sondercommando. After the war, according to my husband, he never talked about the special ordeal he had to go through. I wonder how they managed to prove that they were professionals. We had no papers. Perhaps they all regretted that the Germans believed them, when they started their professions. Cruelty was the name of the game. We all suffered it, but these 'select' professionals must have gone through hell. We heard stories afterwards about members of their families about to get into the gas chamber, in the last moments of their lives, recognising a son, a brother or a husband, and begging them for help. They could do nothing to save their families from the gas that was going to murder them in a few minutes. The only 'help' they could offer was to tell them to move to a certain spot in the chamber, knowing that that was the best spot to die even faster than the rest of the chamber, because the gas came in faster there.

Peter did not want to talk about it ever. No wonder. Every night we witnessed the flames from the gas chambers flaring up into the skies and we smelled the stench of thousands of bodies burning. To this day I have a big problem with smells. I cannot stand my kitchen if I burn a piece of meat. I ask myself over and over again "Why did it happen? Why was it allowed to happen? Why did it happen to us, and was it better for those who died on arrival at Auschwitz or for those who survived?" In fact I question whether there is a God and if so where was He during the Holocaust?

I don't want to write a lot about Auschwitz; hundreds of people have already done that. I will only write about a few of my own experiences as a fourteen-year old.

Our 'home' was for our time in Auschwitz in '*Lager C'*, Barrack 8. We were 1,100 children aged between thirteen and fifteen years. Of that number I believe only 95-100 survived. We were not tattooed with numbers on our left arms, as other victims were, because the plan was that we were soon to die and it would have been a waste of time, money and effort. On our arrival at Auschwitz we were herded into our own special barracks by *Kapos,* who were mostly big, strong Polish-Jewish women. They were real Brunhilda types – like Amazons – and they hated us. They worked for the Germans and were just as cruel. They had food and clothes and even underwear.

We soon learned that there were the *Kapos* and there were us. Those women were powerful – very powerful, and most of them were beasts. The fact that they had underwear was possibly more enviable to us than the fact that they had food. To live without panties was a real hardship for young girls and even today, after all those years; I still can't walk around the house without wearing them. The *Kapos* spoke to each other in a curious German jargon, which we couldn't understand. We later learned that it was 'Yiddish', which most Central and Eastern European Jews spoke. We Hungarians were different even in that – we all spoke proper German. The *Kapos* had a real reason to hate us because they had been in that hell, called Auschwitz, for four, maybe five years by the time we arrived. They were really hardened and we were naïve and didn't understand, straight away, that we couldn't ask them for anything. In the beginning – in the very early days when we still had periods – we tried to ask for something to use as sanitary towels. We received abusive words instead.

There was a toilet block with long concrete slabs with holes in them for our use. We were allowed to sit back to back to relieve ourselves twice or three times a day. It was a real problem if anyone needed to go outside the allotted times and there was, of course, no toilet paper. If a German guard wanted to use the 'toilet' when we were there, he would turn us out – no matter what stage we were at. The Germans always found that highly amusing and had great fun at our expense.

At the very end of the hut in which we lived stood two tall tin buckets, which were to serve us as night latrines. They were emptied and cleaned by a woman who was a Rumanian gypsy. There was a separate *Lager* (section) for gypsies but they were employed in our barracks to empty our slop buckets so they were, evidently, considered to be inferior even to the Jews.

As I write this I find it very strange that we were not expected to empty our own filth, and that the gypsies were forced to do it for us. And yet, at the same time the *Sondercommandos* had to be physicists, professors, architects and priests, in order to move corpses around. In hindsight it is extremely difficult to make sense or logic of any such rules.

The way we were fed was really cruel. At 4 o'clock in the morning the ones 'on duty' had to go to get our 'food'. It was poured into tall, heavy cast iron containers, covered by heavy lids. They had a handle on each side and four of us had to carry each one – two girls behind each other, holding on to the handle with one hand, pushing the back of the girl in front with the other hand so that we did not fall over each other. It was hard work.

Back in the barracks the 'food' was poured into big round dishes, like the old fashioned washing up dishes used to be, and we had to hold it and drink out of it after each other. (Since then, one of the things I never do is to drink out of the same glass after anyone else.)

The food consisted of a warm liquid with bits of turnip, bits of grass, branches of trees, and sometimes even pieces of coal. It was no surprise that we all became skin and bone.

Dr. Mengele – the 'Angel of Death' – made a habit of visiting us almost every day to make his selections. 'Selection' meant that if he picked you out no one would ever see you again. He would stand in the corner and inspect us. We were very young and some girls were very beautiful. We were made to walk, totally naked, in single file in front of him with our arms held above our heads. This would have been bad enough for any person but for fourteen-year-old girls it was a special sort of hell. One evening Dr. Mengele spotted a tiny pimple on the stomach of one of my friends, Lily Biro. She was sent to the infirmary and that was the last we ever saw of her. The Germans cared a great deal about hygiene, the body and perfection, so they couldn't tolerate a fourteen year old Hungarian girl with a pimple on her stomach who happened to have the tragic luck of also being Jewish.

One morning at around 4 o'clock, we were standing for Appel – which was a twice-daily head count – although there was no means of escape and no sanctuary to be found even if we did. The procedure took between one-and-a- half-hours at best and four hours at worst. The worst would happen if a German was drunk and made a mistake in counting us. On the particular morning I write about, I was standing with my friends and I noticed that I had some spots on my arms. The German noticed them too and then we realised that my friend Eva also had spots. We were immediately segregated from the others and put into a separate area at the back of the barrack. It was a tiny space with not even a bunk to sit or lie on, but it had a barn-type door with a gap at the top.

Those unfortunate ones who were put into this space at the back were moved to the 'infirmary' and were never seen again. The infirmary was not used to cure people, it was the last stop; it was the place where one was to stay before being put on to one of the lorries the next night.

I said to Eva, "Listen, we have to get out of here if we want to live".

She didn't dare to come with me, so I left her behind. I climbed over the door and through the gap, and I got back to our bunk where thirteen or fourteen of my friends were sleeping. They were happy to see me and that morning the Germans were looking for me, my friends were all looking for me, and I was looking for me, but nobody found me! That is the reason I survived Auschwitz and Eva, unfortunately, did not.

I have looked back a thousand times to that day and asked myself the questions: did I act in total selfishness in leaving my friend behind, and what could I have done to save her? There was no real choice – I must have used some kind of survival instinct – it wasn't bravery or cleverness, just a desperate need to live. At that time we were closer to being non-thinking creatures, rather than human beings. We were treated like cattle: I was fourteen years old, surrounded by friends who were all in the same inhuman and unbelievably cruel situation. What should I have done? If it were at all possible, I try to convince myself that I would have saved her life too. But it was not possible, and I have to live with that fact.

Some scenes are stronger in my memory that others. Some of the most painful, most terrible times were when some woman from our camp – *C Lager* – would notice a brother, a sister, a friend, sometimes even a husband at the electrified barbed wire fence. She would run to the fence shouting at her loved one, forgetting in the excitement of the moment the danger involved in touching the fence, and then she would drop dead in seconds – electrocuted. Others were more careful and stopped inches from the fence, only to be rewarded for their self-control by being shot by the guards. There was no mercy dispensed to the inmates, no kind feelings ever shown, and certainly no sorrow felt for any of us in our suffering. We were there to die one way or another. It would have been much kinder to have killed us all on arrival.

By this time we 'got to know' the cruellest of men: Adolf Eichmann. He was an SS Officer, a skinny man with a terribly cruel face. We did not know then that he was personally responsible for organising – perfectly – the deportation of Hungarian Jews, right up to the late date of spring 1944, even though the Germans knew that they had lost the war.

Mr. Eichmann 'lingered' in the camp often, but we did not realise what a refined music lover he was.

An orchestra had been formed from the musicians in the camp, some very famous and some not so famous, but Herr Eichmann was a great lover of classical music and demanded to hear it played frequently. The orchestra would sit on the little square just outside the gate of our *C Lager*; we could even look up to see the infamous words – ***ARBEIT MACHT FREI*** – as we listened to the music being played.

There was sometimes an ugly disturbance when a screaming girl, who had just been raped by a German, would be thrown out from a barrack. But Herr Eichmann was so deeply enthralled with his favourite music, from Beethoven or Mozart, or possibly Strauss. These poor musicians were 'paid' by an extra portion of our awful food, maybe a piece of bread with that burgundy coloured 'spread' they called 'marmalade'. We could never find out what it was made of. We knew that the two usual ingredients were not in it – fruit and sugar. Anything else was a possibility. Anyway, the musicians played, and Herr Eichmann listened. A man of his refinement needed to have the best music and he demanded the best available in the very limited circumstances. To say that it was grotesque for us to hear this music is an understatement. We were hungry, petrified, and miserable and the last thing on our minds was classical music.

About two, maybe three times a week (or was it only once?) we were marched to the 'shower room'. They were long stone 'basins' with cold-water taps above them and some awful smelling chemical in the water. This was a disinfectant and we had to dip our dresses in it. Our bodies were placed underneath the cold showers and we were given tiny pieces of soap to use. These were nothing like the soap we used to use back home. Later we learned that the soap was in fact made out of Jewish fat, fat actually from the bodies of human beings.

The skin, human skin was used for nice articles in the German home, like table lampshades, and maybe small stools would also be upholstered with it.

The gold from people's teeth was of course melted down, and hair, human hair was used to fill cushions and pillows. However, they had big problems with shoes because they could not be recycled.

Everything was saved. Everything was very valuable to the Germans, except human life. That had absolutely no value at all.

Guben

The Russians were getting near by October 1944, so the Germans decided to move some of us from Auschwitz to Guben in Germany by train. During that journey the train was stopped and the door of our wagon was opened by a German who pushed in a woman, dressed in clothes that we remembered from the time before our incarceration. She still had her red hair and was Polish – not even Jewish. She didn't talk too much and we all treated her as though she was different from us. She didn't belong; that much was obvious. She was simply different in every way.

We arrived at Guben, which was inside the German border, where we were taken to a small local camp. We were approximately three hundred and fifty women. The *Lagerelteste* who managed the camp was a youngish German female officer who treated us with the usual contempt, but because our work was needed in the Lorenz factory in the town our life there was wonderful, compared with Auschwitz. We worked three shifts making tiny components for aeroplane radios. We had to cut plastic covered fine wire into tiny pieces and make it up into the required items. The colours of the plastic were wonderful and I stole some bits to make necklaces, which I managed, after removing the wire. These I gave to one of the civilian workers in the factory who loved them because times were getting difficult for the Germans at that period, and luxury goods were scarce.

She told me that if I could make some more all the other women she knew would love to have them too. That was when I started my first business with my co-workers and I was paid with bits of bread and sometimes boiled potatoes or other delicacies that I shared with them. The managers of the factory wanted to be nice to us for some reason and gave us a bonus for Christmas, which consisted of some pickled shellfish, which we had never seen before, and some face powder. What we really needed were warm clothes, although by this time we did have some underwear and maybe a pair of stockings. The factory owners needed our work and knew that sick people couldn't produce as efficiently as fit people so our situation in Guben was comparatively good. The officials were not equipped for mass murder, so we all survived.

To return to the red haired lady. One day on the way back from the factory she disappeared – vanished. No one had seen anything, no one had noticed anything strange, and yet she was gone. In the evening the camp *Lagerelteste* made us stand for *Appel* and she warned us that the next time someone escaped the escapee would be executed right there in the camp square. Luckily for us, we still had enough of a sense of humour left to see that she would have to be caught first before she could be executed. As far as we knew she was never caught, but it was so much easier for her: she still had her hair, her clothes and she was able to speak fluent German.

Germany was very cold in winter and my clogs were in need of repair and fortunately we had a cobbler's workshop in the camp, which was run by two ladies who were a lot older than I was. I walked into their room one day and one of them, who was called Vally, looked at me and said, "You are the daughter of Stephie Glasz, aren't you?"

"Yes", I replied," but how did you know?"

"The last time I saw you in Budapest you were about five or six years old. I was a close friend of your Uncle Michael's. We had an affair for eleven years," she answered.

"But why didn't he marry you?" I asked.

"Because I didn't have any money", she replied.

"But did you have any money when you first started your love affair?" I persisted.

She was surprised at this last question. "Of course not!" she responded.

"Then why did he tie you down for eleven years?" I asked.

"Because he was a 'real Glasz,'" she replied, smirking.

(Glasz was my mother's family name before she was married and they were always a mercenary lot, with the exception of my mother.)

After this piece of fantastic luck at being recognised by the 'cobblers' who had known my family as well as my mother, I was given a boiled potato, a piece of bread and a little glass of sweet wine. It happened to be the first wine I had tasted in my life and I shall never forget it. Vally had been the secretary of the Jewish congregation in my mother's home district and Elizabeth, the other cobbler, was a milliner. How they were qualified to become cobblers I never found out and I didn't care. They mended my clogs and after discovering that I was clever with my hands (I had a reputation in the camp by that time for making the necklaces) Vally gave me a piece of black fluffy interlining that was usually used inside the lining of winter coats. It was called 'Vatelin'. They also gave me a needle and thread and I was able to make a pair of leggings for myself. God, I felt so lucky because I was warm and so posh!

In Guben I met up with many women who were from the same suburb of Budapest as my mother's family. Among them was a very nice-looking young woman called Zsoka who was married to a Dr. Schwartz and had a little boy. I didn't know her before and knew nothing about her until one evening, my saviour, Vally, invited me to a party. It was not the kind of party that we know – there was no food, drink or entertainment. The women had made a special table out of a square piece of paper that they had laid out on the floor, and they had drawn a large circle on it and had written the letters of the Hungarian alphabet around the circle.

Suddenly, someone produced a button (I think it must have been the cobbler ladies because they worked near the stores), and the button started to move from one letter to another making up whole words. The words became sentences and we believed a spirit was talking to us. The button spelled out a message for Zsoka telling her that because she had let their little boy go with her mother back on the railway station in Auschwitz their son had perished straight away. It told her that her husband would blame her and would never forgive her, and that she was never to go back to Budapest because her life would be in danger.

Some weeks later we noticed that Zsoka had a pair of soft brown, real leather lace up shoes. They were even her size. A little later she was wearing a taupe, knitted wool suit. We also noticed that one of the bosses, Herr Muller, was doing her little favours.

Anyway, one day as we were being prepared for our move from Guben, Herr Muller took Zsoka away from the camp and no one knows to this day where she went or what happened to her. We all wondered though whether Zsoka took the warning of the spirit seriously or whether she fell in love with Herr Muller, or both. Her son was indeed gassed with his grandmother on their first day in Auschwitz and her husband did survive and returned home, where he later remarried. I became his patient and when he learned that I was in the same place as his wife, he told me that he was heart-broken when he heard of the death of his son, but that he'd never stopped loving Zsoka. So you see, the message had only been partly right!

The time was now early January 1945, I think, and the Russian guns were making their unmistakable noises, coming closer and closer and rumours were circulating around the camp that we were to be moved. Vally said one day that she had found one knee-length sock and a ball of wool in the storeroom. She asked me if it would be possible to make her a pair of socks, out of the one sock. I gathered my 'co-workers' together and we went foraging amongst the trees, breaking off thin branches to make knitting needles out of them. After cutting the one sock into two halves, I picked up the stitches and started to knit the foot part of the other sock.

We knew by this time that we had only one day left in Guben, and as I was knitting the lights went out due to an air raid so that the already difficult task of completing the sock became almost impossible. The needles kept breaking as they dried out and they had to be replenished often. My friends told me to give up but I made a bet with them that I would finish the sock and so I did, by the light of the moon. You can imagine what this masterpiece looked like, but it was wonderful that Vally had a pair of warm socks to wear during our two-week forced march across Germany through freezing forests and harsh snow-covered countryside in the middle of an extremely cold winter.

The original sock was machine made, out of a soft dusky pink, sort of heathery wool. But the little ball of wool was a dreadful shade of acidy green. Good thing that my sense of colour was not as finely developed as it is now! It would have bothered me while I was working on it. Of course, I am only kidding!

We were on our way to Bergen-Belsen. During that march which lasted fourteen days, we were given ten-minute occasional breaks, and I can remember leaning against a tree and sleeping for eight minutes out of the ten – which might have given me the extra energy that I needed to survive such a journey – who knows?

We had very little clothing (we had managed to get panties in Guben) and wooden clogs. The hard snow accumulated beneath our soles, which meant we had to chip it off frequently. It made walking very difficult. We huddled in barns and outhouses trying to shelter from the bitterly cold nights and the local German farmers gave us some food – hot soup made from beetroot or carrots with bits of bread. Anything was better than the appalling muck, laced with Bromide, which we'd been given in Auschwitz. We were reacting badly to the withdrawal of the drug, which had kept us acquiescent and mensturation-free for so long and so, like deprived drug addicts; we suffered from 'cold turkey'. The Germans, you see, couldn't cope with the messiness of young menstruating girls – it wasn't hygienic. We became nervous and agitated and were not placid any more. There were two sisters with us, who were normally loving and inseparable, but they started to fight and many mornings we noticed that they were bruised and had actually drawn blood. Sadly, both of them perished later and I don't know where or when. There were three to four hundred of us on that march and we all survived it to my knowledge. The SS guards marched us through German towns, but no eye contact was made between the locals and us as we passed through their streets.

CHAPTER FIVE

~ Bergen-Belsen ~

Bergen-Belsen, after Guben, was a terrible shock. There were thousands of rotting dead bodies lying around and these were piles of bones covered with parchment-like skin outside our huts. The stench was unbelievable. There were no bunks, and we had to sleep on filthy floors with one lice-infested blanket per person. Food was even scarcer than in Auschwitz and we were only fed once a day. I learned that the word 'awful' had degrees. The food was awful in Auschwitz but in Belsen it was most awful. We existed from the end of January until the middle of April somehow and the last two to three weeks were even more than 'most awful'. We were given some hot liquid and that was all. People were dropping dead by the minute and I don't remember any sort of sanitation or ever having a bath or shower in Belsen.

Auschwitz had been a well-organised 'showcase' for the Third Reich. The system functioned with clockwork precision and here the Final Solution was almost perfected. Auschwitz was, almost, the perfect killing machine, but by the time we were rotting in Belsen Germany was losing the war and the country was falling apart. Belsen, therefore, having been deserted by the high officers and left to its misery, disease and infestations, was the hell that nightmares are made of and the cruelty there was incomprehensible to most of Mankind. There was no hospital and the people started going mad with brain-cell destruction due to starvation – I am convinced this happens. We sat or lay around on the ground outside the huts every day. There was nothing to do, nowhere to go and no energy with which to do it in any case. There were those infamous stinking piles of dirty naked bodies – skin and bones that everyone has seen in photographs and films. Sometimes I would see a pile move because someone had been thrown onto it before she was dead.

We would sit around talking as best we could but nothing happened to us there so there was nothing to talk about except that the older women, who by this time had lost touch with reality, repeated over and over again what they had done in previous birthday parties for their children or spouses. One day, a friend of my late mother kept on baking imaginary chocolate log cakes with all the trimmings and leaves out of imaginary sugar. She made the icing in two different chocolates to make it perfect in her eyes. Those poor ladies would bake their cakes one day, and be put on the pile of bodies the next. Listening to them, I remember promising myself that if I ever survived that hell I would never let anyone who was around me in my future home go hungry and I have kept that promise and, even if I have no money, I always have food for everyone.

Susie, Steve's cousin who had burned herself in the ghetto in Keszthely, and I were together in Auschwitz, Guben, and also Belsen, where only one hut separated us. I was healthier than she was towards the end so I went to see her every day. I was in love with her cousin and she was in love with a boy we both knew from our town. In Belsen we were just lice-covered skin and bones but we still hoped and planned and daydreamed about the future. Then, on 14 April 1945 – the day before our liberation – I went to see Susie but she wasn't there any more. A little later I found her lying on top of a pile of bodies outside her hut and that was how I saw her for the last time. She would have been far better off if she had died from her burns in the ghetto in Keszthely than to have suffered as she did in Auschwitz and Belsen.

My poor, poor Susie. The woman who had slept next to her gave me Susie's blanket. It was covered with lice.

On the 11th or 12th April 1945, Belsen was quiet. There were no Germans shouting around the place – they had all suddenly left – they had run away. We felt nothing: we were numb and too far gone to realise what was really happening. Then on Sunday, 15th April 1945 (to this day I do not know how we knew the date, but we did), I saw a vision through the filthy windows of the hut as I was sitting with my back against the wall. A British jeep appeared though the glass with two young soldiers. They were followed later by other British soldiers in war vehicles. The miracle had happened.

I could just about stand so I went outside and saw the British soldiers. I spoke to the first officer in German and thanked him for liberating us. They climbed out and stood there in disbelief at the unexpected scenes of horror with which they were confronted. I learned later that many of them had to move away to vomit before they could gather enough strength and courage to face us and that those young soldiers, who had seen quite a lot of fighting, death and mutilation, were overwhelmed by the sight of us.

In a short time they had started to bake bread. We were in desperate need of food – there was no doubt about that – but their kindness combined with freshly baked bread, cold baked beans, with bacon and sausages was too much for stomachs that had been deprived of food for weeks. Hundreds died. The 'Brits' had done their best to help us but it was too late for so many.

Shortly afterwards they entered the barracks with DDT guns (the miracle powder of the '40s) and sprayed us, and within minutes there was a 2-3cm-thick grey carpet of dead lice covering the floor. We fell in love with those wonderful British boys. I remember wondering if they hated having to touch us: they didn't show it even if they did. They were there – the British Army was there – and they couldn't do enough for us. It was admirable that they could do anything after the shock of seeing us, but we didn't realise that at that time. What they saw on entering Belsen were thousands of emaciated, rotting bodies with flesh-pierced skin, flies, filth and devastation: what they smelled was the stench of the remains of people. Those young men fed us, created showers with running cold water – the fact that the water was cold was a minor detail after what we had been through – it was such a luxury to be able to wash at all. They talked to us and we felt as though we were in paradise. I spoke no English but managed with my German to make myself understood and I also managed to understand that they intended getting us away from that place as quickly as possible.

On the second or third day of freedom I went outside with the others to look around and because I was so weak I fell into a great hole that had been used for storing potatoes. Immediately a British soldier ordered a former SS guard to lift me out. It was a terrifying moment – I thought the guard would throw me back into the hole or hurt me in some way – but he valued his life too much to risk hurting me in front of my British liberator. (Some of the guards who had fled from the camp had been caught and made to work by clearing bodies and generally cleaning up the camp. Some were killed in the fury felt by the soldiers).

It was about this time that we were told that a very famous British broadcaster and journalist was going to come and see us and sure enough this distinguished person appeared with his microphone and photographers. He was visibly shocked by what he saw and the photographers took hundreds of photographs as they walked around the camp. We had no idea who he was and I only realised that it was Richard Dimbleby when I sat watching a television program on the 20th Anniversary of the Liberation of Bergen-Belsen in my Cardiff home. I had seen Mr. Dimbleby many times on British television but it was only then that I recognised him as the man who came to Belsen on that day. I have listened many times to his original message, which was broadcast around the world in his stricken voice.

"*This day at Belsen was the most horrible day of my life. I saw it all – the furnaces where thousands of people have been burned alive – only stunned before they were packed three at a time into the flames. The pit – fifteen feet deep - as big as a tennis court, piled to the top at one end with naked bodies so emaciated, with yellow skin drawn so tightly over them that they looked already like skeletons. The British bulldozers – digging a new pit for the hundreds of bodies lying all over the camp days after death – untouched and unburied. The dark huts, piled with human filth in which the dead and the dying are lying together, so that you must step over them to avoid the sticks of arms that are thrust imploringly towards you".*

A few days later the Lord Mayor of the town of Belsen was brought to the camp with a group of Germans. They were amazing people. The camp was only a few miles from the town but not one of them knew of its existence. Some of them looked as if they were in a state of shock and were unable to look at us – the almost dead – let alone the dead. By that time the SS guards who had been rounded up had been forced to remove the bodies from the mass graves and had taken them away so that there were fewer bodies lying around for the townspeople to see. There was, however, enough evidence for those Germans who wanted to see to accept what their own nation had done to so many innocent men, women and, worst of all, children of all ages.

A few days after the liberation we were moved to the actual town of Belsen, which was originally built as a Hitler *Jugend* training camp. The town contained houses that were mainly three to four storeys high – real houses with rooms and stairs and bathrooms. There was still only cold water but it seemed like being in heaven. We wandered around the town suburbs in order to find food. The food we were given was never enough to assuage the hunger we felt and we were never certain of having food the following day. We were to remain in that state of mind - fearing starvation – for a very long time after returning to normal life. We were also given pieces of soap – at that time we were not aware that the soap we were given had been manufactured from the fat that was taken from the bodies of Jewish victims.

I remember one day walking around the home of a German family who were sitting in the kitchen eating and I saw a silver spoon in a glass on the window ledge. Although I had never stolen anything in my life, I took the spoon without hesitating and put it in the sack that I had used for scavenging potatoes that day. We had lots of uncooked potatoes and onions but nothing on which to cook them. Now it makes no sense but then it meant security to people who were no longer capable of thinking rationally.

A short time after the Liberation, the Americans took the camp over from the British and gave us a packet of cigarettes a day. I didn't smoke but I took them all the same thinking that they would come in useful for something. I think that was the best move I ever made in business in my life because, soon after that, when we were being fed regularly, cigarettes became hard currency and their purchasing power was incredible.

My friend Kathy's mother died 3 days after the Liberation because no doctor came on that day. I became ill during that period but I was very lucky because it was the day on which the doctor made his rounds in my particular building. (Many had died because they were taken ill on the wrong day when there were no doctors available.)

I was transferred to a hospital where I was told that I was suffering from Typhoid Fever. The doctors prescribed a diet of milky tea, which, in my mind, was another form of starvation, and the smell of hot cooked meals that were served to the other patients was too much – they made me even hungrier. One day I became yellow all over – even my eyeballs were a deep golden colour – and then even the small amount of milk I had been given was forbidden me. That same day they brought dinner for the rest of the patients, which happened to be German sauerkraut containing big pieces of fatty pork.

"Please may I have some?" I begged the nurse "Certainly not", she replied, "it would kill you".

I got hold of a Polish male-nurse and started to negotiate with him about the sauerkraut and that was when my cigarette allowance became hard currency. I think it cost two or three boxes of my finest American Pall Mall, but I clinched the deal with him. I ate a bowl of food that, medically speaking, should have killed me, but instead I recovered and my colour changed from revolting yellow to almost normal. I think that was the most delicious meal I'd eaten since the time I left my home in Keszthely.

I feel that I am extremely fortunate because I came out of that hell reasonably well. I am almost healthy and I don't cry when someone questions me about Auschwitz and the war. I can laugh and I feel that life is very important to me and yet there are things that would reveal to an analyst the underlying torments that lie deep within me. I have some obsessions that I am sure originate from my time in the camps. I always lock the door when I go to the bathroom because communal showers taken with hundreds of women, with German eyes always watching our nakedness and personal activities, have certainly affected me. It was degrading to say the least to have no privacy during my maturing years, but to have it taken away in such a brutal fashion was a very cruel experience and it has left me scarred.

Looking back I try to remember Dr. Mengele's eyes and his facial expression and I wonder whether he had sexual fantasies when he watched our young bodies filing past him every day. Some of the girls were exquisitely beautiful and sexually attractive – at least in the first few months before they became skeletons – and they must have looked interesting to any man. We didn't find out if Mengele took part in the rape sessions that many of the German guards were involved in, but with his power he could have amused himself in any way he wished, privately or otherwise. The guards drank and raped the inmates at will – it was part of their normal behaviour and was recreation for them.

I haven't mentioned Irma Grese until now. She was known as the 'Queen of Death' and was always able, willing and ready. She was German, blonde, blue-eyed and deadly. She had a very striking appearance and always wore a light blue man's shirt, a divided skirt and shining brown leather boots, with a leather thong whip protruding from the right one. We never knew when she would turn up but some time every day she would put in an appearance and when she did she never hesitated to use her whip on some helpless person who had unwittingly annoyed her, and then she would beat them until they were dead.

We had all watched her abuse those poor people. They were powerless and submissive as she stood over them. She showed no mercy and flogged them with a detached expression upon her face as though she was performing any normal household chore. We who were terrified of her stood in silence – paralysed with fright wondering whether we were to be her next victim. It was difficult to say whether she was crueller than Mengele, but because she was a woman her cruelty was unexpected, somehow it was hard to imagine such a degree of evil in a woman. I think Hitler must have been extremely proud of her achievements in killing so many Jews – if he knew about it. Even today I cannot look at that colour blue without thinking of Irma Grese. It is a colour I detest and I cannot work with it. I'm not too fond of leather whips either.

Irma Grese was captured her arrogance must have stopped her from trying to escape. These people were so superior – so "*Deutschland, Deutschland uber alles*". Most of them felt too proud to think of escaping and what was worse was the fact that they didn't even think they had done anything wrong. I've not thought of Grese for a long, long time, but now I am forcing myself to because I want to write about her and her part in my life.

In evidence at the trial of Josef Kramer and 44 others held at the British Military Court, Luneburg that started on 17th September 1945 Brigadier H. L. Glyn Hughes, C.B.E., D.S.O., M.C. said:-

"Shortly before the 15th April, 1945, certain German officers came to the headquarters of 8th Corps and asked for a truce in respect of Belsen camp. In pursuance of the arrangement arrived at, he went on the same day to Belsen camp, after it had been captured. There were piles of corpses lying all over the camp. Even within the huts there were numbers of bodies, some even in the same bunks as the living. Most of the internees were suffering from some form of gastro-enteritis and were too weak to leave the huts. The lavatories in the huts had long been out of use. Those who were strong enough could get into the appropriate compounds but others performed their natural actions from where they were. The compounds were one mass of human excreta.

Some of the huts had bunks, but not many, and they were filled absolutely to overflowing with prisoners in every state of emaciation and disease. There was not room for them to lie down at full length in the huts. In the most crowded there were anything from 600 to1000 people in accommodation which should only have taken 100. There were large medical supplies in the stores at Belsen, but issues for the use of the prisoners were inadequate. The witness had made a tour of the camp accompanied by Kramer, the Kommandant of Belsen; the latter seemed to be quite callous and indifferent to what they saw.

The principal causes of death in Belsen were lack of food and lack of washing facilities which in its turn led to lice and the spread of typhus. Even after the liberation matters were not easy in the way of food, in spite of the facilities which the British had, because special feeding was necessary".

Another witness, Major A. L. Berney stated that he arrived at Belsen on the 15th April. The next morning he went in search of food for the Belsen internees to a Wehrmacht camp which was about three kilometers up the road. There he saw a Hauptmann, who said that Belsen had been supplied from his stores. Major A. L. Berney said that in the store at the camp there were 600 tons of potatoes, 120 tons of tinned meat, 30 tons of sugar and more than 20 tons of powdered milk as well as cocoa, grain, wheat and other foodstuffs. There was a fully stocked and completely staffed bakery in the Wehrmacht camp capable of turning out 60,000 loaves a day.

During the trial proceedings, survivors provided extensive details of murders, tortures, cruelties and sexual excesses engaged in by Irma Grese during her years at Auschwitz and Belsen. They testified to her acts of pure sadism, beatings and arbitrary shooting of prisoners, savaging of prisoners by her trained and half starved dogs, to her selecting prisoners for the gas chambers. She habitually wore heavy boots and carried a whip and a pistol. She used both physical and emotional methods to torture the camp's inmates and enjoyed shooting prisoners in cold blood. She beat some of the women to death and whipped others mercilessly using a plaited whip. The skins of three inmates that she had had made into lamp shades were found in her hut.

Thirty of the accused were found guilty; Josef Kramer and Irma Grese were amongst those sentenced to death by hanging. The death sentences were carried out on the 13th December 1945.

I was still in the hospital in Bergen-Belsen and being visited by my two wonderful friends, Vally and Elizabeth, when a delegation from the Swedish Red Cross came into the room.

"We are taking some survivors to Sweden to recuperate", announced one of the delegates.

"Then I can be one of them," I suggested.

"That's not possible at the moment", I was told. "You're far too weak – your weight is only 25 kilos and you'd never survive the journey. We cannot take the responsibility – at the moment it would be too much of a risk".

"Please, I know I'll be all right – if I survived everything else I've been through, I can survive a journey to Sweden" I pleaded.

They looked hard at each other, not knowing how to deal with such a determined desperate child, and then one of them suggested "Well, if we discuss it with the medical staff they might have some views".

They called in eleven doctors for a consultation regarding my fitness to travel. They consisted of a mixture of nationalities. There were Poles,

Swedes, Czechs, Austrians and others I don't remember, and all had the benefit of a medical degree. To this day I do not know how they could prove what qualifications they had, but genuine or not they agreed that I could go but only if I signed a waiver absolving them from any responsibility if I were to die. I had to work hard to convince Vally and Elizabeth to sign the papers too, because they were acting as my guardians, and because I was only fifteen years old they were asked to sign *in loco parentis*.

I said goodbye to Vally and Elizabeth and all my old and new friends and was put into a small ambulance and transferred to Lubeck docks. At the docks I had to be carried from the ambulance to the ship over the shoulder of a former SS guard and, as he carried me, I was filled with terror – that indescribable terror once more – and I truly believed that he was going to kill me. I remember saying to myself: "Why doesn't he throw me in the water, he knows I am too weak to swim."

I don't remember the distance we covered, nor do I remember the time it took us to cross that space, but I do remember the helplessness I felt, to this day. I was petrified and then I hit my head into something and my heart thumped mercilessly until I was safely on board. He didn't kill me and I often wonder why he didn't.

There were, I think, three small ships waiting for their very strange passengers to board. We were emaciated, with a little hair starting to grow; we had no luggage and not even a change of underwear. I was placed on a spotlessly clean, beautifully equipped, small, immaculate Swedish ship that became my transport to a New World. The staff consisted of doctors, nurses, cooks and cleaners. The Swedes were wonderful; we had hot water, white clean sheets, pillowcases and towels with which to dry ourselves. We had soap that smelled so fragrant after the stench that still hung in our nostrils, and toothbrushes, toothpaste, nightdresses, underwear and decent clothes to wear at last. We were given chocolate and fresh fruit, and were treated gently and with care – as though we were human beings and not animals. At the beginning it was difficult to believe all this was happening to us. It was also difficult to get used to seeing normal, lovely looking people who smiled and who wore white uniforms – with not a whip in sight. They spoke softly to us, no one shouted; there was no more abuse and we were on the road to recovery at last.

What material was I made of? I was fifteen years old; I was twenty-five kilos in weight and still had some fight left in me, even after Auschwitz,

Guben, Belsen and Typhoid. Maybe I was a born survivor – people have often told me so.

It was June when we left for Sweden. The journey was a revelation and we were amazed at the northern lights, the light nights and the breathtaking scenery. We went through the Gotta Canal with its hundreds of fascinating, colourful islands – some with only one house on them. It was like being in an unreal dream after experiencing a grotesque nightmare. On the first morning a nurse came in to my 'room' and said that if I wanted to I could eat 35 breakfasts, because everyone else was seasick, except me! Amazing! One of the doctors asked me whether I could see any good resulting from the tragedies of such a terrible war that had caused so much suffering to so many innocent people. I said then, with my fifteen years of wisdom, that I hoped that the world had learned a lesson, but now, fifty years later, I feel that it has learned nothing. A very eminent British historian told me that I was too pessimistic - I do hope that I am wrong and he is right.

However, arriving in Stockholm was like another miracle. We were taken around in a bus to see that splendid city before being taken to an old town called Sigtuna. There we were to occupy a lovely Girls Private School during the summer holiday. It had been made into a temporary hospital for us.

The trip in the little white ship and the caring, professional treatment received from the nurses and medical staff began the miraculous process of healing my frail body. The stay in the hospital where they were determined to improve my general health and make me put on weight was something else - I went from 25kg to 60kg in seven weeks! They were very worried that I wouldn't survive and took a great deal of trouble with my food, as well as giving me two-hourly injections of vitamins and liver extract. I became chubby, but I was alive, which was far better than being skinny and dead. I cannot remember much about the people I was with at that time – it was a long, long time ago and a miracle that I managed to regain my health at all.

After having been in Sweden a few weeks the Red Cross visited us and showed us lists of other survivors who had arrived in Sweden and I was delighted to see Vally's name on it. She had also been brought there by boat shortly after my own arrival.

Many of the nurses in the hospital were voluntary workers and, amongst them we soon discovered a very beautiful actress called Vera Waldor whose stage name was Unger. She was not only gorgeous but she was a very nice person as well. I wanted to give her a present to repay her for her kindness but, of course, there was no money available. I eventually obtained some cotton wool and gauze from one of the staff enabling me to make her a little gift, but because the material was so limited, I too was limited in what I could make. Just prior to this period, the Jewish Congress had sent some people to us to enquire what our needs were regarding writing paper, books, sewing needles and thread etc., and they had sent us what we had requested. I borrowed a pair of scissors and begged some cardboard boxes and made my first and only heart-shaped embroidered handkerchief or jewellery box. It was padded with cotton wool and covered with gauze. I even made a card somehow and presented it to Vera. She was delighted and some time after this episode, when I visited her in her apartment, I was thrilled to see my little gift in pride of place amongst her beautiful antiques in her very elegant home.

Later that summer we were told that the school would be restarting so we had to vacate the building. We were then taken to Ronninge for a few weeks. By this time I was well enough to go out on my own and instead of going to a collective place near Malmo; I chose to go as an *au pair* to a Swedish family who lived near Stockholm. This was also the time that we received news from home. The International Red Cross had been looking for missing persons and I was still hoping to hear some news about my father, who would have been forty-two by that time, and my beloved Steve. There was no news.

I met a girl from Nyiregyhaza, Hungary who was also a survivor and whose name was Clara Spitz. Clara was a talented violinist and was friendly with another girl called Agnes Kaufman, who was a talented pianist. They were both two years older than I was. They met a famous musician whose name was Dr. Charles Garaguly and who was the head of the Konzerthuset (Concert House) in Stockholm. Dr. Garaguly was originally, I believe, from Hungary and he offered Clara free private music lessons. She must have been very gifted for such a man to pick her out from the crowd. Agnes and Clara had a little spot on Swedish radio on Christmas Day, which was a great honour for them, and subsequently Clara was offered scholarships to two American Colleges of Music. She could have had a great career for herself but unfortunately it was not to be.

In Ronninge I met an old friend named Elizabeth Lazar, from Keszthely. The two of us had sat next to each other in school for eight years. Meeting her was like a miracle. We were the same age, we had the same colour hair, and we had ‘art’ in common. Liz was a good sketcher.

Somehow we managed to meet in Stockholm during the next month. I remember one of these meetings taking place in the beautiful apartment of Mr. & Mrs. Izbicky. They were German Jews who were lucky enough to come to Sweden in 1939. They had made it to freedom, but no other members of their family did.

They were happy for themselves and sad for their relatives and were nice to us. Then Liz and I went to different countries – she to Israel and I to disaster in Hungary. We met again in 1993 on my visit to Haifa, where she lives happily with her lovely husband Gerson, a Hungarian University lecturer. We had a short visit but old memories were coming back. We are now writing to each other and hope to meet once more.

Liz was the daughter of a lovely couple in Keszthely and had a brother called Joseph. No one except Liz survived. Not only did all three of them die, but also she does not even know when or where. What gave the right to these Nazis to take away the chance to visit the graves of the parents, siblings, and grandparents? And there are people, even the British – a few – who deny that there was an Auschwitz, that there were gas chambers and crematoriums.

But back to 1945 and Sweden.

I worked as an au pair for a family called Nordlindh. Mr. Stig Nordlindh was a civil engineer and his wife Maxine was an American whose mother was a Mrs. Leonard – the widow of an American Post Master General.

There were three children in the Nordlindh household: Denis who was four years old, Catherine (called Kitten), who was three, and baby Christian, who was eighteen months old. I was employed to look after them and help a little in keeping the house tidy. By the time I realised what was happening I was in charge of the whole household, and at fifteen I was doing the cooking, washing (with the first washing machine I had ever seen), ironing, cleaning (the house was large) and shopping for the whole family. At the time I didn't resent doing all the work – I was thankful to be alive and to be living in such comfort. I was young and spoke reasonable German so found that learning and speaking Swedish was a fairly simple task and in a matter of weeks was teaching the baby his first Swedish words and sentences.

I have a funny memory of Sweden, which was the time when I was sent into Stockholm to buy special German bread (Tyska brod) and some cheese. I didn't realise how smelly the cheese was until I noticed people moving away from me, and I sat on the bus in a void as I travelled towards the railway station. Luckily I realised that it was the smelly cheese they wanted to avoid and not me!

Lillangen where we lived is very near to Stockholm and the house was on the edge of the sea with the water only thirteen steps away from the garden. The summer there was beautiful and the winter was exhilarating, with diamond–glistening snow covering everything in sight beneath a brilliant sky. It was clean and silent and I loved the majesty of it all. I used to go shopping to the village pushing one of those sledges that looked as though it had a rustic chair fixed on to runners, and I would propel myself along with one foot whilst the other rested on a ledge at the back, or I would slide downhill with both feet on the back as free as a bird. It was great fun for a fifteen-year girl who had had no enjoyment for a year and a half and I can remember strapping Christian on to the seat and flying down to the shops.

When Christmas Eve arrived that year Mr. Nordlindh piled us all into his car and drove us to church for the Midnight mass. He parked the car and I remember walking through knee-deep snow on a clear, moonlit, winter's night and its beauty overawed me. In the little church there were lots of people sitting, praying and singing hymns. They were surrounded by burning candles and they were people who hadn't suffered during the war. In that respect Sweden was different from almost all other European countries. The Swedes were either lucky or clever. Now we know that Sweden's neutral state was not so neutral and that Sweden had been clever in serving both the Nazis and the Allies at the same time, but back in 1945 I didn't know that. All I knew was that I was most probably an orphan and that I was lonely and forlorn, but oh how I remember how magical that Christmas Eve was to me – yes, it was beautifully, beautifully magical.

That evening I thought about the previous Christmas and the time spent in Auschwitz, Guben and Belsen and about the German people themselves. I thought of the sad state in which we had been – with no hair, no food and no decent clothes to cover our poor bodies and I wondered also about the state of our tortured minds. Nobody cared then – really. I was destined to have died and I kept asking myself what had prevented my death. How could the Christmas of 1945 have been so wonderful in that beautiful free country of Sweden, when just a year before life had been so totally grim and hopeless in Germany? Had we been completely without hope then, I kept thinking. Did I ever feel that I would not survive that hell I'd been thrown into simply because I committed the unforgivable sin of being born Jewish? Why did I have to pay such a price for something over which I had no control – like my birth? Questions about hope mounted in my mind and then I realised that I'd never really lost it and that I must have been one of those incurable optimists or just too young to understand.

Maxine Nordlindh told me about the 'terrible hardships' they had endured during the war.

"Don't think for a minute that we didn't have problems here," she said. "Do you know that for six weeks we couldn't get any cream at all and we had to drink our coffee with milk? There was no butter either for the same length of time, and we had to use margarine as a substitute".

My heart still bleeds for those poor Swedes, especially when I compare them with the people of London who were bombed continuously and the British people as a whole, who coped with severe food shortages throughout the war, and even after it for several years.

Christian is now in his early fifties, he is six foot four inches tall and like his father is an engineer. Mr. Stig Nordlindh is ninety-five years old and lives in the south of France. He remarried after losing his wife many years ago when she was sixty. His second wife has also died but he is not alone because he has a lady friend who is eighty-five years young. He still drives a fast sports car around the roads of southern France and sometimes gets into trouble for speeding!

Three years ago I went back to Stockholm and with great pleasure visited the NK (Nordist Companiet) department store and, naturally I began to think about my life with the Nordlindh family in 1946. They loved to eat grilled sardines for dinner – it was one of their favourite meals. Unfortunately it was one of my jobs to buy tiny, fresh sardines, slit them open and sprinkle their insides with a pinch of salt and pepper and stuff each one of them with parsley. This was quite irksome, as you may imagine, because with at least seven people to feed (each person would eat on average fifteen sardines); I would end up stuffing dozens of little fish. Of course I didn't eat with the family, being the hired help, but had my meals in the kitchen, which must have been a bit annoying after all, that preparation.

Some time during my stay in Sweden I got in touch with Vally, who without any doubt helped me to survive and for whom I've always felt a deep gratitude because of what she did for me in Guben. She lived in Stockholm at that time and some matchmaker had introduced her to a lovely orthodox Jewish man, whom I had the pleasure of meeting some years later. She must have been very fond of him because she studied hard to become an orthodox Jewish wife to her husband-to-be, who before the Holocaust was an orthodox Rabbi in a big town in the Romanian part of Hungary. He'd had a wife then and five children, but only he had survived. After long months of learning, Vally was ready to take on the difficult role of the lady of an orthodox household. She learned well and became a totally dedicated wife.

One day Clara and I actually went to the Stockholm Opera House to see - and mainly to hear – Verdi's Aida. It was a first for both of us. It was magic, a mesmerising experience. At that time we didn't know yet that the tenor role: Radames was sung by the world famous Jussi Bjorling, a native of Sweden. Aida has certainly awakened my interest in opera and I have not stopped loving them.

I had decided by that time to go back to Hungary. I desperately wanted to see my father and Steve and longed for news of them. Hope of finding anyone alive who had not already returned home was running out and there was still no news of my father. A few days before we were to leave Sweden to return home to Hungary Clara phoned me and said:

"I don't need you to take presents back to Budapest for me, Mady, I've changed my mind and decided to go home too, and will travel with you."

CHAPTER SIX

~ Return to Keszthely ~

We went back to Hungary from Sweden in 1946, hoping that we would find our loved ones. What a terrible mistake – what a terrible decision we all made that day. We gave up a heaven for another hell.

We had no one to give us advice; we were very young, very lonely and very hurt by what had happened to us and didn't have a clue about what lay ahead of us, so we got into the train and said goodbye to Sweden and the Swedish people. We travelled through Poland. Eastern Europe looked very sad the year after the war ended. The people looked downtrodden, they were badly dressed and poor; buildings had been destroyed and food was far from plentiful.

We arrived in Budapest to find that it was no better than the other places through which we had passed. I was greeted at the railway station by my uncle Geza and his wife, and I knew the minute I arrived that I had made a terrible mistake. They took me to their house in Kispest, which is a suburb of Budapest, where they gave me a room and some food. The next day they took me to see a friend of theirs who had two shops selling porcelain, glassware and household goods on the main street of Kispest. The purpose of the visit was to get employment for me and I started work there almost immediately, and although I hated it I had no choice but to do it. Later on I was to go back to school.

My uncle told me that he had met Steve in Buchenwald and that Steve had told him he was there with his father, who'd had a lame foot for many years. My uncle – my blood relative – my mother's brother – who worked in the kitchens in Buchenwald and had access to food, even if it was only a turnip or potato, told me that he had not helped Steve because "he wasn't aware of the seriousness of our relationship".

"You were too young to have been committed," he said.

So poor Steve and his father had perished. I heard later that Steve had given what little food he had to his father, thinking that because he was young and strong he would make it. He did not survive. I believe my life would have been so different if he had not been another of Hitler's prey. But he was not as lucky as I was.

Whenever people ask me how I survived, I always say that the Final Solution wasn't perfect, although the Gestapo engineered it very carefully. The machinery worked well without too many hiccups for too many years, but in the last few months of the war the Germans started to realise that it was all over, and, as time ran out for them, they failed to complete the task they had set themselves of killing all the European Jews. They had to leave the job unfinished and couldn't cope with the thousands of emaciated bodies lying in open graves. There was no one left to bury or burn them, and those of us who managed not to become corpses were nonetheless living corpses.

Those of us who managed to move about without food for weeks – those few of us who managed to live to tell the tale – realise that we were Hitler's mistakes. It is a tragedy that he made so few, but nothing is ever perfect, is it?

In Keszthely we had been around one thousand Jews in a population of ten thousand. I think 90 – 95 people returned from the most horrendous hell man has ever created for man.

George Cziffer, Steve's friend who asked me to go out with him in 1942, must have got over the terrible disappointment of being turned down by me, and grew up to be a real lady's man! He was one of the very few young men to survive the Holocaust and he returned to Keszthely, studied medicine in Budapest and eventually qualified to become a TB specialist. He was the only child of wealthy parents who loved him dearly. His father was the only wholesale wine merchant in Keszthely. Mr. Cziffer did not return but their loyal housekeeper kept much of his estate intact for George, who was very talented and whose career as a doctor was full of promise. Unfortunately he died in his forties from an illness he'd brought back with him from the camps. He was labelled 'the most likely man to succeed' when he was a young man and had brains as well as talent in the sporting world and was a champion swimmer – but he was not greatly endowed with luck. I remember the terrible shock I felt when I heard about his untimely death.

My Uncle Geza managed to smuggle his wife, who was seven months pregnant with their second child, out of the camp where they were held in June 1944 by bribing a non-Jewish friend. She was given false documents and taken to live in the countryside with some decent peasants whom they paid for looking after her. The new documents had transformed her from Mrs. Glasz to Miss Kovacs. A few weeks after her release she gave birth prematurely to an illegitimate (due to the false papers) weak little girl called Judith in the basement of a hospital. They stayed in the country with the peasants until my uncle returned from Buchenwald.

At the same time that my aunt went into hiding, my grandmother and my uncle's nine-year old very precious son, Gabor, were also interned. My uncle paid for them to be released the day after my aunt, but forgot to instruct his mother not to return to her home in Kispest. A few weeks later at 2 am, they were rounded up once more by the Hungarian Gestapo and taken to Auschwitz, where they were both gassed on arrival.

In 1945, after the liberation, my uncle returned home, and instead of finding his wife with their ten-year-old son, Gabor (whom he had groomed even at that tender age to be his successor in his business), he found her with their one-year-old daughter and blamed her for the death of their son. He was a simple though very clever Jewish man for whom a son was more valuable, more important and more useful than a weak, sickly girl who, on top of everything, had to be legitimised. It took a whole year. The papers were all right but his heart was not. In the summer of 1946 they had another child whose reason to be born was to be a replacement for Gabor, but turned out to be a girl too, whom they named Susan. Although he wouldn't admit it, he never really forgave Judith for being alive when Gabor was not. Susan became his favourite. She was more fortunate than her sister and became a solicitor and married a doctor and had two very clever sons. But Judith's marriage, which had not been a success at any time, fell apart and her daughter was not held in the esteem that Susan's sons were. Tragedies never end and my aunt who had developed heart problems during her year in the country passed away aged fifty-eight. My uncle lived for over twenty years after her death but never got over the loss of Gabor.

My mother was one of five children; Charles was the eldest and my mother was the youngest. Charles went to live in Havana, Cuba, in the late twenties and made a good living there from the timber yard that he owned, but he must have felt homesick and lonely without his family and decided to go back to Hungary. He settled in the part of the country that became Czechoslovakia in a small place called Szencse, where he opened another timber yard and married a lovely, intelligent, softly spoken girl called Ethel. She was blonde, blue-eyed, good-looking, slim and well dressed. He took his bride to Venice and Florence for their honeymoon and in time she gave birth to two sons, who were named Thomas and Ivan. They were all taken to Auschwitz and they all died there. The decision my smart Uncle Charles made was an even bigger mistake than the one I made on returning to Hungary from Sweden. He was a grown man whereas I was a sixteen-year old child.

Earlier I wrote about my friend Lily, who died because she had a spot on her stomach. Of course she might have died later on from some other cause like starvation or typhoid, but at the time of her death we were terribly shocked. Her death happened at the beginning of our stay in Auschwitz in July 1944, and I returned to Keszthely in July 1946. I visited some survivors and amongst them was Lily's poor father. He was only in his early forties but he was a broken man who had aged far more quickly than he would have done under normal circumstances. He made me welcome but a few minutes into my visit he said to me "Mady, you were such a good friend of my Lily – why didn't you send her back instead of you?"

I sat there stunned, feeling accused of something – everything seemed so unreal after all I'd been through, and I realised that I still had a lot of learning to do. I had survived, yes, but only to hear those words. Mr. Biro was a very nice, intelligent man, who was well educated but had been destroyed by the loss of his beloved wife and two daughters, one of whom was Lily. Again, their only crime was to have been born Jewish.

Mr. Biro remarried like so many others who had lost their spouses and families, and sought comfort with another survivor who was formerly a Mrs. Slovak. Those tragic, sad people got together to try to create a new life for themselves, and to try to forget the past, but I don't think any of them succeeded in doing so. Losing a child is unnatural, but losing a whole family under such circumstances is something with which one can never come to terms – it's all too much to bear. Mr. Biro and his new wife had a few weeks of happiness after the end of the war when her son Stephen returned home. The happiness, however, was short-lived because he died aged twenty of some terrible disease he had caught in the camps and the second Mrs Biro died of cancer shortly after. Mr. Biro could take no more and ended his own life. Hitler's vision of ridding the world of Jews started with such passion, continued long after his death and long after the war ended. In fact, will it end while some of the survivors are still alive? Maybe not...

I have already stated that my stepmother Manci and her sister Florence perished and I never found out where, and that her wonderful sister – the one I called Aunt Sarah – and her twelve year old daughter perished immediately on their arrival in Auschwitz. But there was another sister called Irma who was a stunningly beautiful woman and quite a remarkable character.

Those years were like the Middle Ages in Hungary, and there was no such thing as having a child if you were not married. But Aunt Irma fell in love with an attractive man called Dr Marton. He was nice and handsome and all would have been perfect, except he was married and his wife would not give him a divorce. So Aunt Irma had an illegitimate son called Stephen. Dr. Marton adopted him so that at least the boy had his father's name. As if that wasn't a big enough shock for the families and the whole town, two or three years later Aunt Irma gave birth to another boy whom she called Tibor. Dr Marton adopted him too. Later one of the professors from the Agricultural College married and made an honest woman of Aunt Irma and from then on not only did she live in luxury, but she even had one of those Hungarian titles which are given to people for doing something special. Dr Keller, her husband, became something like Dr Sir Oscar Keller and, consequently she became Lady Keller. Stephen became a lawyer and Tibor a surgeon and during the last twenty-five years of his life Tibor became the most famous surgeon in the whole of the country. He specialised in cancer and achieved wonderful results. He also became Professor of the Medical University in Budapest. He once told me that Keszthely, although a tiny place had excellent schools and had produced a great number of very talented, well educated and highly qualified people.

Lady Keller had been taken to Theresienstadt – one of the less cruel camps – and had managed to survive. After her return Dr Keller, who was a pure Aryan Christian, could not get over the undignified, humiliating treatment his wife had received at the hands of the Nazis. He did try very hard to save her from being taken away in the first place but even a man as prominent as he was could do nothing to stop the German Project and he never came to terms with that fact and he died a very hurt, insulted man.

I have spoken to everyone in Keszthely who came back from the camps. I always hoped a mistake had been made about Steve and that he might return home from somewhere some day, but all I have left of him is one of his school photographs that someone found amongst the papers of the priests who had taught him. (So many of those wonderful priests died too, either at the hands of the Nazis or the Communists, and church schools were closed too, first by the Germans and then by the Russians.) I never discovered how or where my father perished, but I did learn that he was dead. I sincerely believe that my poor thirty-one-year-old mother was the fortunate one because she died of natural causes way back in 1937, ignorant of the evil that I would be forced to witness. She was so beautiful and had such a zest for life.

Dr Andrew Rosenberg – our GP who disappeared long ago in my story – had three brothers; Paul who became a barrister and who is still alive and in his nineties, Michael who was killed in a bomb attack in the Ukraine, and Joseph who was a civil engineer and worked on the railways and was my father's friend. With Andrew already gone, and Paul (who also had a doctorate in law) in the labour camps, their mother Mrs Rosenberg was extremely worried about Joseph, her third son. They expected him to be called up any minute, but a terrible tragedy saved him from deportation and almost certain death. He was standing on the railway measuring something or other when one of those four-wheeled inspection trucks sped past and accidentally amputated the front parts of both his feet. He was kept in hospital for several months and no one knows how the authorities forgot about him, but they did. He survived and died an old man long after the war was over.

Everything good and worthwhile in Keszthely was ruined – even the beautiful palace of Prince Festetich – and with penknives people cut pieces out of the exquisite handmade tapestries. They defecated on the beautiful chairs that had been so carefully carved by craftsmen and stole everything that was moveable -–even the old wood-block floors that had been made years before and which had been kept in perfect condition for so long. There was hardly anything left of value after the Russians and the locals had finished with the place. Everything was removed for souvenirs or more likely for firewood and, if the war-stricken people were so poor and so desperate for firewood during that extremely difficult period, who can blame them for taking what they needed? But it was sad to see such beauty destroyed.

One day after my return to Hungary and after I'd lived there for a while something strange happened. My uncle, who manufactured Soda Water, used horses for delivering it to his customers, and one of his horses became sick. The local vet was called out and I had a real surprise when I recognised him as the vet, Dr Kamaras, who had practised in Keszthely before the war. He was a stunning looking man – we always thought he should have been a movie star – and his wife was very attractive too. She was tall, cool, blonde and they had two daughters who were just as gorgeous as their parents. Mrs Kamaras used to be a good customer in my aunt's shop and I remembered the knitted suits she used to order. When I saw Dr Kamaras coming to the back yard to examine the poor horse I called out to him. He looked at me and said:

"Oh my God, Mady! You came back!"

I'm sure he was quite pleased – he was not a nasty man – but the shock of seeing me was undeniable. He in fact tried to say something pleasant, and said:

“Do you know, since Mrs Hoffman went, I can never get that wonderful string I used to buy in her shop”.

He then proceeded to explain that he needed the string to castrate female pigs. With this strange statement he managed to get rid of any odd feeling I might have had had after witnessing his reaction to seeing me. It did make me feel, however, that our return must have caused some strange feelings amongst the Hungarians who were left in their homes when we were so cruelly taken from ours. They were still leading normal comfortable lives as though nothing had happened when we returned. I feel the decent ones must have felt some little guilt at least, but the Nazis on the other hand must have thought that a mistake had been made. They could not have expected to see us again once we were deported.

There were those – not very many – who actually gave back the items that the Jews had left in their safe keeping in 1944, but sadly the majority denied ever having received anything at all and were visibly annoyed at seeing us back on their streets.

We had lived in Hungary for generations, we had been well integrated, we had done no harm to anyone, we believed that we were part of that country and its people whom we loved, but they betrayed us so tragically.

After my return to Hungary, in the summer of 1946, I remember having to go into town to buy a comb. My aunt counted out money – all paper notes – several notes in several ‘different colours’, put them in a shopping bag – they were so many – and told me that it would be enough for the comb, my bus fare there and back and an espresso coffee. By the time I got into town, the inflation went up so much that I could not have a coffee. Inflation was rampant. Hungarian money was worthless. People with real money were exchanging dollars; the Black Market was busier than ever. People were bartering everything and the rich were getting richer, while the poor had no chance. My uncle came home on several occasions, bringing smaller (or larger) pieces of diamonds – an emerald or two sometimes – I remember one of these pieces; it actually was a part of a diamond tiara. We were wondering to whom it used to belong? It could have been just some rich lady, who, like so many others, found herself penniless. It could even have been a member of the Hungarian noble families or the aristocracy.

In the summer of 1946 I returned to the little town of Keszthely. We the returnees were all housed for a short time in a building that had been used as a sort of cultural meeting place and a home for various charities before our hell began. The building was called (translated from the Hungarian) 'The House of Love'. It was a nice building with a huge main hall with either one or two (I don't remember) floors built around an atrium where we could walk along the corridors and look down on to the main hall.

One day we were standing on the first floor looking towards the entrance when we noticed an unusual disturbance. Not knowing what it was we went down to investigate and saw a tall, very handsome elderly man with long white hair and beard. He was dressed in the typical blue cotton trousers and jacket that the French workmen wore in those days. He walked into the building, followed by a boy pulling a four-wheeled cart (there were still no taxis or buses) on which were stacked three big suitcases. We then realised that he was a local Jewish man, Mr. Berger, who had disappeared in the early thirties. The story was that Mr. Berger and his wife had a textile shop on the high street and that he had gone to Budapest one day in 1932 ostensibly to buy stock for the shop but had never returned home. He had disappeared and the Danube had been dragged even in the search for him. Everyone went to the capital to buy wholesale goods for their businesses – there was nothing unusual about that – but to vanish so mysteriously, that was very unusual. Mr. and Mrs. Berger had a gorgeous son called Louis who was in college when this happened. His parents had wanted him to become a professional violinist, but instead he became a professional actor and changed his name to Basti, and after the war he started to become very successful. (During 1942 he was in a labour camp with my father).

Basti was tall, blonde and blue-eyed – he certainly didn't look Jewish. So, when Mr. Berger walked into the House of Love on that summer's day in 1946 everybody was in a state of amazement, maybe even shock.

"Does anyone have news of my son?" he queried.

"He's fine, don't worry. He's a famous actor now and lives in Budapest. He never got himself a wife, though", somebody informed him.

"Would you like us to send a telegram to let him know you're here? We asked.

"No thank you – there's no rush – tomorrow will do" he replied.

He was silent at that last remark and although we were all very surprised that he didn't need to see his son immediately, we felt that if he'd waited 14 years to see him one more day would make no difference. I think that all those years before, it was because of Mrs. Berger he had run all the way to France and after she died he decided to return home. But how did he know that she was not alive any more? We all wondered.

The telegram was sent to Budapest and the next day Louis (Lajos) arrived by train and he walked across the town from the railway station to the House of Love wearing a short-sleeved summer shirt. His tan enhanced his good looks and with his blue eyes and blond hair people forgot he was Jewish – or maybe they all tried to forget what had happened on the same station in the same town two years before. They certainly celebrated his fame that day. He was overwhelmed by it all and especially by the meeting with his old father who had left so many years ago and whom he thought dead. They went to Budapest where Louis wanted to take a flat for his father, but the old man's wish was to live in Keszthely, where he had lived before going to France. I saw Louis a few times and when I asked him why he'd never married, he said, "Mady, my mother was mad, my father is mad, and I'm sure I am too. Why should I make some nice girl miserable?"

But he did get married eventually to a very young actress who became restless and they soon divorced. Then he married a nice lady who bore him a beautiful daughter who became a great actress in Budapest. I saw Louis play the part of Vronsky in Tolstoy's 'Anna Karenina' and I was thrilled as he took the part of the man whom Anna fell in love with and who was the cause of her downfall and death. His acting was superb, the cast was wonderful and I enjoyed it all the more because it is one of my favourite novels. But that was a long time after the event I am writing about here.

That same summer, when I was in Keszthely and living in the House of Love, I visited the teacher, Gabriella Kovesi, to whom I'd said goodbye in 1944 – the one who said; "I'll see you again".

She was elderly by that time, a spinster and extremely poor. She lived with her very old mother in a rented flat because she had never had enough money to buy property of any kind. She was genuinely pleased to see me, and I promised myself that I would help her, somehow, if and when I could ever afford it.

I still have my friend Marta (the one I used to meet every morning outside my aunt's shop in Keszthely). She is a year younger than I am and is living in Budapest. Her parents, Mr and Mrs Weisz, were a very attractive, tall handsome couple. Her brother John was a very large boy already at thirteen, so large in fact that his father had to take him to Budapest along with the local cobbler to get custom-made lasts to make shoes for him. He was very tall, very good-looking and very strong. We all loved and respected him and because of his size there was more of him to love and respect.

Marta's mother, Lenke, was a beautiful lady, a wonderful mother and a good housewife and cook; she was everything in fact that was expected of a nice Jewish woman. The family was healthy, well respected and loved by all of us – it seemed secure and indestructible. Marta and her mother were together for a while in Auschwitz until Dr. Mengele came and decided that Mrs Weisz was no longer good enough for his purposes – whatever they were. Marta to this day blames herself for not begging for her mother's life. Mr. Weisz and John died together, probably during bombing raids – Marta is not sure because she never received any confirmation of how they perished and no one received confirmation of how people died.

Marta went home from the camp riddled with Tuberculosis and because her spine was badly affected she had to remain in hospital in Budapest and was nursed on a plaster bed for four years. During her stay in hospital she met a lovely man called Paul who needed surgery to his lungs during which process some ribs had to be removed. The surgery left the right side of his chest shorter than his left but eventually the TB was cured. He and I always talk about the possibility that somehow our dreadful time in the camps made us stronger and maybe even more resilient to hardships.

An uncle of mine used to say when we wanted to be a little sick, "There are only healthy Jews and dead Jews – there is no such thing as a sick Jew". I often wonder if he learned that from Hitler himself.

CHAPTER SEVEN

~ The Occupation of Hungary ~

The Russians were occupying the country after the so-called 'liberation'. Liberation was the wrong name for the new nightmare that had just started for the folks of Hungary. It was almost expected that this little rich country would again have a bigger power to 'look after' it as it always did. There were the Romans, the Turks; there was the Austro-Hungarian Empire. There were the Germans and almost immediately the Russians. The political situation was impossible. The first party to fall was the Social Democrats. This must have been around 1946-47.

In 1948 the Hungarian Communist Party took up the lead power; total power; one party only. A terrible little man, Comrade Rakosi, became the head of the new government. Everything was nationalised. People lost their businesses. Individuality was fast going out of life. People were afraid of everything. They were afraid of the government, of the secret police, and even of their friends and neighbours. A strange system started to work whereby a student 'made it' to college – university – not by his intellect, or his achievements in school, but his background mattered. If he or she was the son or daughter of an intellectual, or of a middle-class parent – he or she could not get into higher education. One had to be a good 'kader' to get in. A good 'kader' was the child of a peasant or labourer. This system was deadly. People fell out of universities but only if they were really hopeless, or if the lecturer dared to get rid of them, in spite of their 'perfect' background. Otherwise they somehow qualified. They became bad doctors, bad architects, and bad engineers. Of course this was not because they came from working or peasant 'classes', but because they were not qualified for the occupation they had been pushed into.

The terrible house shortage was partially solved, not by building more homes, but by dividing people's houses or flats. The size of the house was measured. It was then decided that the family who owned it (and who had probably lived there, in some cases, for generations) would keep only a room or two, dependant upon the size of the family; the rest would be given over to needy people who were homeless.

Remember the wonderful film 'Ninotchka' with Greta Garbo? (and the newer version 'Silk Stockings' with beautiful Cyd Charisse). Both of these films showed the terrible way people lived in Russia. Whole families put into one room, sharing the kitchen, bathroom and toilet with – sometimes – dozens of strangers. This was not only unfair and inconvenient, but in many cases dangerous. Just like in the films mentioned earlier, they couldn't even talk freely in what used to be their home. Enemies were all around. Neighbours reported each other for even listening to the BBC News, whether it was true or not, just like in Nazi times. The Hungarian 'KGB' called 'AVO' might 'call' on you at 2am, take you away and if you were really unlucky, you could end up in Siberia with a life sentence. People disappeared. In most cases they never even found out what their 'crime' had been.

People were also afraid to wear a fur coat that they had owned for years because their enemy might start rumours. This in turn could generate reasons for an investigation, which could end up badly, only because you had a good coat and couldn't or wouldn't (and indeed why should you) say where the money came from for it.

While I was in Keszthely I tried not only to find my Jewish friends, but also the Priests, the Professors who used to teach Steve and my other friends, all those long ago years.

The priests were gone; no one knew what had really happened to them, but according to the local people, some of the priests were rounded up by the Russians, some just disappeared. (Here we go again, I thought). Now, after the Germans did a good job in getting rid of the hated Jews, it was the turn of the new group – or groups to be hated and chased out of their homes and even their country.

We knew that the landowners, aristocrats, noble families and priests/nuns would be punished, for the feudal system was still in operation in Hungary until the communists reorganised everything.

The fate of the priests was sad. They became the enemy of the new system, because the Soviet regime did not recognise religion. All religious activities were banned. Church schools were closed, and churches abandoned. This was not the fault of the priests, the same way as the fact that Hitler hated the Jews was not their fault. Nevertheless they had to pay, and how they paid…

Hungary has never really enjoyed democracy. In 1948 when the communists took over, new waves of horrors started.

The huge inflation ended by the drastic new laws the Communists introduced; the new money came into use.

The feudal system was finished. Farm workers couldn't work for landowners any longer, because they had to walk away from their land. These poor people, who had suffered terrible hardship over generations, now believing the promises the Communists kept on making, were hoping that at last they would have their own land to work on. They were hoping to produce from their land and to finally have a decent life at last.

This sadly did not happen. These tragic people who never had anything, who had always worked so hard, were now 'organised' into so-called 'Co-operatives'. On the face of it – at least for a while – it looked as if the peasants would have a better life. The system was similar to the Russian 'Kolhoz' where people worked three times as hard as ever before, where they had to produce exactly what the government dictated, and in return they were just as poor as before. Not only was the quantity too much for these people, but also it was even too much for the soil; not to mention the primitive way in which these poor people had to work.

The co-operative had no modern machinery – remember the way the Russians worked their land? I think they still do work their land this way. Whatever machines were doing in developed countries, people and a few unfortunate farm animals had to do in the 'Glorious Soviet Union' and its 'Satellite Countries'.

These people, who in normal circumstances could have fed the whole of Hungary, didn't even have enough to feed themselves and their children. However, if they could not reach the required 'quota' they had to 'buy in' milk, wheat, and eggs, whatever they were ordered to produce to meet the requirement of the State. They had no money, and no food left. They were disappointed and disillusioned to say the least.

Politically you couldn't win. Marta's cousin, a highly qualified professor of Economics, was a Communist ever since his university days. He was one of the true classic Communists, the real intellectual who supported all that Mr. Marx and Mr. Engels wrote, and what many students wanted to believe. It sounded wonderful: equality; equal rights; equal chances, equal pay etc. Tragically, Mr. Marx and Mr. Engels left out one tiny ingredient: human nature. It is impossible to start out with ten young men, same trade, same age, same family – (wife and two children), same income, house, etc. However, it is impossible to keep them the same, for within six months all these families will be totally different.

For instance, Marta's cousin Alexander (Sandor) was informed by Comrade Rakosi that the Communism that Sandor believed in was not the Stalinism our occupiers were practising. Mr. Engels never mentioned the awful crimes that Comrade Stalin was going to order his henchmen to practice.

Sandor was in a camp in Hungary for several years, where due to his terrible ordeal he became not only ill but also a manic-depressive. Several years later he weighted his pockets down with stones, walked into the Danube where his body was found days later and 20-30 miles further down from Budapest. The tragedy was even more immense as by this time he was married (to the daughter of a prominent minister in the government) and had a young son. His suicide, his tragedy was not the only one; it was just the one closest to us.

Everything that came from the West was considered dangerous. For people who had relatives in America, or England, receiving 'care packages' was like Christmas. Unfortunately, by the time they actually received the parcels everything that was of value, good quality and considered useful would have been confiscated; only the rubbish remained. I have to say that some relatives had no idea of what we actually needed, and in many parcels there were such things as beaded, sequinned evening dresses, ostrich feather boas, and other totally useless items! What we needed were clothes. We had very little because money was in short supply and even if you had some to spend there was nothing to buy.

The shops were practically empty and supplies came in very erratically. Sometimes there was a shipment of sugar; the news came and we all would run and buy sugar, after having stood outside the shop for hours. Another time we heard that the store had received one hundred brassieres. Once inside, we paid our money, received a ticket, and then went to the 'pick-up' place to collect a brassiere. Size did not come into it! Within minutes there would be 100 women, each with a brassiere, trying to swap theirs with each other. Some, I think were even lucky enough to go home with a brassiere that actually fitted! In the case of shoes, this was the same story. We had to queue for bread, flour, etc., etc.

One good thing was the irrepressible sense of humour of the Hungarians, as shown by these jokes:

1. Husband goes home in the middle of the day and finds his wife in bed with his best friend.

   Husband to best friend: "Your wife will be very angry when she finds out that you were making love to my wife instead of standing in the queue for lemons"!

2. Very long line of people standing for hours for bread. Little old man at the back cannot stand it any longer and tells his friend that he is going to the other building where Comrade Rakosi's office is and he will kill him.

   A few minutes later he comes back. His friend asks what happened. The little old man replies: "The queue is even longer over there"!

3. 8-year-old children are taught in school that Comrade Stalin is their father and Comrade Rakosi is their mother. In answer to the question: "What would you like to be?" the 8 year old replies, "Teacher, I would like to be an orphan".

There were some good things too. For instance, medicine, hospital treatment, and maternity leave - all were socialised, free.

A special perk was a fortnight's holiday with full board in beautiful parts of the country for the 'workers'. These holidays took place in beautiful villas, hotels that were originally mansions that had belonged to the rich before they were 'nationalised'. In other words they were taken by the state without even penny compensation to the owners. This was awful for those who owned these beautiful places before, but excellent for those who now enjoyed their annual holidays in them.

The famous '5 year plans' were useless. Nothing was built. There was no money spent on even repairing or restoring the beautiful old buildings that were damaged during the war.

Very few people had cars. It was mainly the Party Leaders who enjoyed the luxury of being picked up and delivered in a car with a driver. The rest of us travelled in the streetcar and on buses. During rush hour the scene was not unlike those we see from India; people hanging on the steps of the streetcars like bunches of grapes. It was awful. I remember hanging on to the rail of a bus, on the outside, while pregnant. People couldn't help even if they wanted to, because the bus was just too crowded.

During this time a strange type of shopping developed. 'Dollar shops' were opened where those few who were paid by a foreign government – American, British, German, etc. – could shop with their foreign – hard – currency.

There was a famous Hungarian fashion designer who was allowed to keep a very exclusive salon open in the middle of the most beautiful street in Budapest. She was called Clara Rothschild – related to the famous Rothschild family. Miss Rothschild was the only person who was always allowed to travel to Vienna, Milan and Paris to buy exquisite fabrics for her expensive and very 'high couture' gowns and dresses.

The reason for this was that she created the kind of garments, which were desirable enough for ladies like Farah Diba, the wife of the Shah of Persia (now Iran), for movie stars and also the wives of famous people. More importantly these celebrities also came into Budapest, and Miss Rothschild was able to sell her creations for hard currency. The country was starved for negotiable currency. Hungarian money was not worth anything outside the Hungarian borders.

The situation did not really get much better after Stalin's demise; although some people managed to get back their permits to start – re-start – small businesses.

With a permit you could employ one or maybe two helpers, but this only made a difference to very few. My uncles – and my aunt – all managed to get back their permits and again started to manufacture soda water, which was the business they were always in.

(I should mention here that after 1948 when the businesses were taken away from the small – and large – private businessmen, my two uncles took employment in the businesses, which they had owned before, but were only called in, some time later after the 'State' had ruined them all. The original owners managed to drag the bankrupt businesses up and had them running again.)

In Communism there is no unemployment. Every job was filled by two or three people; they could afford it because salaries were so meagre. I remember a friend visiting me in New York who worked in one of the ministries. She was going to spend three months in New York. When I asked her what would happen to her job, she replied with "It will be alright, because there are another two people who can – and will – do my work."

The communist idea kills every kind of initiative. I was visiting in the early 1960's and walking around the big lake – The Balaton. I was watching a man holding a garden tool with a long handle, doing something in the garden of one of the holiday villas. I asked Marta why he was taking out only one weed in every five minutes. Marta answered with "Why should he work any faster, he will not get any more money if he kills himself with speed".

But, back to the ten horrible years of 'Building Communism'. I had a job in the Ministry of Planning, where three thousand people were pushing thousands of pieces of paper. Phone conversations took place; we were distributing building material, which the country did not have. Plans were worked out for new buildings, which never materialised. Buildings were pulled down, but not rebuilt. After work, I think two evenings a week we had to stay in the office buildings to attend Communist Seminars. They tried to teach us the glorious story of the glorious Soviet ideology. These evenings were boring and tiring. We knew the ideology was far different from the reality. These evenings were the only time in my life when I smoked. The smoke of the cigarettes burnt my eyes, and kept me awake.

There was one remarkable 'perk'. There was no income tax – no one could pay it in any case. Most goods went to Russia. Where was the money coming from? It wasn't coming at all; the coffers were drying out. In 1953 Comrade Stalin had been dead for several days before we were officially informed. Secrecy was the Soviet's strongest weapon. We, who listened to the BBC, knew that the mass murderer of millions of Russians had died at last. Who would follow him?

An unbelievable thing happened. After it was made public that Stalin was gone, his critics came forward and he was criticised for all the years – 25 in all – and he was named the cruellest mass executor; the most ruthless of all dictators. I remember being at a meeting – a sort of neighbourhood gathering – and when they opened it up for questions (after telling us what a horror the Stalin era had been), I stood up and asked how it was possible for the millions to tolerate this monster during his decades of being in power.

This was soon after Stalin's death. My cousin, whom I was with, kicked me in the shin to make me shut up. We did not know yet if it was safe to ask a question like that. Anyway, the answer was "Everybody feared him". Millions and millions of Soviets and other millions in the western countries were all afraid of one man. He practically bankrupted the US with the armament they forced themselves into in preparation for a Soviet attack. Alas, the West did not know that the Russians were almost penniless and there was no money for the poor tragic population, after the fantastic size of the forces was kept up.

Was this a repetition of the Nazi era, or maybe just a continuation? The people who were unlucky enough to live in those countries just 'swapped' the dictator. Hitler for all those terrible years and now Stalin for other terrors. Many of the Nazis just swapped their colours and became Communists. (Now after so many years, many of the old Communists are the biggest capitalists.)

By the time Stalin died, everyone was poor and desperate. During his regime, agriculture, a very important part of the 'total Hungary', was pushed into total ruin.

The 'farmers' were paid pennies for the foods they managed, and the black-market – again – was forced on them by the government. If they wanted to be able to buy shoes for the children, they had to sell some eggs, chickens or cabbages on the quiet. They were ready to revolt.

CHAPTER EIGHT

~ The Uprising ~

After my return to Hungary in 1946, I found my paternal grandparents had, miraculously been saved by Raoul Wallenberg. He was a wonderfully brave Swedish diplomat.

Mr Wallenberg had worked in a bank in Haifa in the mid-thirties, where he met some refugees from Hitler's Germany. Later he worked as a foreign representative of a European company run by a Hungarian Jew. Hitler's occupation of Hungary in 1944 made life for the Jews – 700,000 of them – very dangerous and Mr Wallenberg was sent as a 'diplomat' to Budapest and was assisted by the Swedish and American governments to help save Jews, somehow. He designed a Swedish protection passport and arranged 'Swedish Houses' that offered refuge to Jews and managed to save around 100,000 of them.

That man was the only man dedicated enough to do something. No one else did – even the Vatican was silent.

Raoul Wallenberg was taken by the Russians after the Soviet occupation of Hungary in 1945 (they called it liberation!) to the Soviet Union and no one really knows what happened to him – he just disappeared. After a great deal of hard work by his family and the Swedish government in trying to trace him, the Russians said that he died in the infamous Lubyanka prison of a heart attack in 1947, but witnesses stated that he was in prison until the 1970's.

It is an irony that the anti-Nazi Comrade Stalin, with his vitriolic propaganda about the wonderful Soviet Union's freedom and equality for all its different peoples, felt the same way about the Jews as the Nazis did and imprisoned the only person who dared to do anything to help them. The only Champion of the Hungarian Jews had been forced, therefore, to suffer in terrible prisons that, we learned, were no better than the Nazi concentration camps.

The Americans gave Mr. Raoul Wallenberg honorary citizenship in 1981 and the Canadians gave it to him in 1985. The Israelis were late in honouring him and left it until 1986 when they planted a tree in his name, which still grows in Jerusalem. I wonder what took them so long. There is a statue in his memory in Cardiff, too.

It is not easy after all this time to write about these memories. I have read a number of books and watched a number of movies about the subject of the Holocaust and they all have something new to say. Sadly Auschwitz or Bergen-Belsen has become 'yesterday's news', so what I've tried to do here is write about people I knew, many of whom I loved and almost all of whom I have lost.

During the years of 1950 –1953 I was working at the 'Ministry of Planning' in Budapest, responsible for the cultural life of the three thousand or so people who worked there. We had no money, our salaries were pitiful, but we could all afford to go to the theatre and opera because it was cheap. In the 'socialist' regime all cultural projects were heavily subsidised by the Government. So I went along every so often and 'purchased the whole house'. The Hungarian Opera House seated (if I remember correctly) between 1100 – 1200 people. I bought all the tickets, for example, for the 'Nutcracker Suite'. I purchased 'the house' in smaller theatres for plays, classics and modern. Of course I went to see everything I fancied. They played Shakespeare and Moliere. I saw Shaw's Pygmalion and Tolstoy's Anna Karenina and everything in between.

Those days the Russian Ballet was very prominent. Several young Hungarian ballet dancers won scholarships to the Bolshoi or the Kirov and had the chance to study with the best. The Ballets we had the pleasure of watching on Hungarian stages were second to none. We saw the well known classical ballets and the then new Russians productions.

During this time two young, very promising students of the ballet were sent to Leningrad to study at the Kirov. Their names: Nora Kovacs and Istvan Rab. They returned to Budapest fully qualified and became top dancers at the Hungarian Ballet. Nora was prima ballerina and Istvan was famous for being able to 'fly' over 3 – 4 male dancers, who squashed together on the floor, in some of the modern ballets which were all choreographed by the leading ballet masters. The two of them – both very attractive people – decided to remain in either London or Paris – I don't remember – after a tour. The Hungarians were very shocked, at least those Hungarians who believed in 'building socialism'.

However, I was twenty-two years old when I met and married a non-Jewish Hungarian who was eleven years older than I was. He was divorced and we worked in the same place and I married him against everybody's advice. I continued to live with my husband in the part of my uncle's house that I had bought out of money I had inherited when I first returned to Hungary. We were married 5th November 1952 and had absolutely nothing in common. We were two entirely different people with completely different interests and outlook on life, and it was a disastrous marriage from the start. I think I married him to get away from my family's obsession with money and I lived to regret it from the beginning. In fact, before my daughter was born I had already filed for my divorce – it was that bad.

We had no money, but then nobody did in those days – and I had to support my daughter because my husband brought home very little money. During my pregnancy I learned to design knitwear and use a knitting machine, and that was how I began my career in fashion.

When the baby was born I called her Ildiko, the name of the wife of Atilla the Hun, Ildi for short, and I nursed her on my left arm and controlled the knitting machine with my right hand. I obtained a divorce in 1955, after great difficulties, and was on my own for one year with my daughter before the Hungarian Revolution took place. I remember getting off the streetcar after I received my final divorce papers. The walk took about 5 minutes from the streetcar stop to my uncle's house, but it was long enough for two friends of my family to approach me with some very interesting offers. Both of these men were married, but obviously interested in 'setting me up' for a life of 'comfort'! Basically they both said that if I were 'willing' they would rent a little flat and give me 'an allowance' which would make my life 'easier'! I was shocked and of course refused. When I told my uncle about his two friends he was surprised.

I, like all the Hungarians, managed somehow, but the situation in the country did not improve. We had no choice, but then something very important happened.

One nice day in October 1956, the big uprising started. I went to the theatre to see Bernard Shaw's 'Saint Joan'. As we were walking up to the theatre, there was something strange going on in the city.

There were hundreds of young people – students and others – all over and looking different, excited. I actually met an actor I knew, who was sitting on the top of a tank. He called down and said "See you in the Sacher next Thursday". The Sacher was – and is – a very famous hotel in Vienna, with an equally famous 'patisserie', coffee shop which makes the 'Sacher Torte', the wonderfully rich chocolate cake covered with a shiny chocolate top and the two layers put together with delicious apricot jam. (I did not take too much notice of his invitation for coffee in the Sacher, which was just as well, because I could not have made that date.)

Anyway, we watched Shaw's masterpiece and were totally engrossed in it, so much so, that the part of the play where poor Saint Joan is put on the stakes, some loud noise sort of 'disturbed' us – just a little – but we honestly thought that the sound came from the fire – on the stage.

As we left the theatre, big crowds were going all over the place. The town was very noisy. There were no streetcars or buses any more, only noise and people. But then, walking in the direction of the outskirts where we all lived, we realised that dozens of men were dragging heavy parts of what looked like a statue. In fact these big heavy pieces of a statue used to all belong together, creating a huge Stalin, our beloved Father who had been dead for three years.

Hungarians were celebrating the first taste of freedom, or what they thought would be freedom. By the time we walked towards the Radio Building, we heard that that the 'revolution' had taken it over. There was some shooting, lots of running and shouting. A kind man stopped his car – seeing my old aunt walking with us with difficulties – and gave us a lift home.

The first days were wonderful. Hungarians chased the Russians out. There was, of course a full-blown Revolution by this time – cruel members of the 'AVO' – the secret police – were executed, mostly hanged. People were seeking revenge. Eleven years of the Russian occupation was enough for Hungary. The people wanted freedom.

The Russian troops seemed to disappear. Hungary gave out a big sigh of relief. We are free! But not for long. A few days' later Russian tanks and other vehicles, and troops – it seemed like millions of them, all returned to the little country, which, because it was rich, they wouldn't give up so easily. The new Prime Minister – Imre Nagy – sent a SOS message to the Western World for help. "Help us, please help us", but no-one came. It was the tragedy of the Hungarian uprising, that the West was too occupied with the Suez Crisis. It was more important, bigger business, bigger money.

The Russians started to fight the Hungarian Revolutionaries; there was a house-to-house battle going on and the little country didn't have a chance against the huge Soviet Union.

People fought with what they had. 'Molotov Cocktails' (bombs) were thrown from windows on to the Russian tanks. These tanks were dreadful. We were scared days and nights. We did not know how it would all end.

Marta had longed for children and had started to work at it. She became pregnant but couldn't carry the babies to full term. She miscarried a few times and then she became pregnant again in the early part of 1956. She longed for a little girl and wanted to call her Kathy. That year during the revolution the telephone wires were out of action so that there was no means of communication.

We knew that the people in Budapest, six miles away, were hungry and couldn't even get bread. There was no transport available so everybody had to walk everywhere. One day I was standing in a queue to buy bread when a Russian tank opened fire on us. I wasn't hurt and luckily I managed to get two large loaves for Marta and Clara. I started walking to the city. As I did so I saw several crushed bodies of people who had simply been in the way of the Russian tanks. Eventually I got to Marta's flat, but found that she had been taken to hospital and that Kathy had been born, so I walked a further two miles to visit my God-daughter to be and said my goodbyes to Marta. I gave her the present for Kathy, as a good godmother should. I delivered the other loaf to Clara and told her too that I was leaving.

CHAPTER NINE

~ A Journey to the Future ~

When the first opportunity came to leave the country, Ildi was in the city with her father and I couldn't contact him immediately – there being no means of communication as I stated earlier. I got hold of her eventually.

A group of us paid someone to take us by truck from Budapest to Sopron, which is very near the Austrian border. We had all made up our minds to escape from Hungary, despite the fact that we had no 'papers', and so we sat on the floor of a truck with boxes of meat piled up all around us. On the way we were stopped by Russian soldiers, who shone their torches into the truck, but luckily they did not find us.

My little three-year-old daughter was so quiet and frightened that I couldn't even hear her breathe. We arrived in Sopron and because we had to cross the border at night the driver dropped us off and we were on our own. They took us only as far as they felt safe. These were professional 'people smugglers'; they knew the territory intimately and would not risk their own skin.

We all met and set off but five minutes after our escape attempt we were picked up by the Russians. Everybody who had tried to escape that night was caught because the wind was blowing in the wrong direction, and all the sounds of our movements were carried straight to the Russians. We were all taken back to the city and to the *Comandantura,* which was in a grand old building used at the time as the Soviet Army Headquarters. It deserved a far better fate.

The very old people who had tried to leave Hungary that night and parents with young children, like myself, were given pieces of paper, with a number on each one and the Russians stamped these with a rubber stamp. Ironically the Russians had chosen the very hotel where four years earlier I had spent my honeymoon. Holding the hand of my little girl I stepped outside the building in order to walk to the hotel, which I think was called Pannonia, and my daughter said, "Mummy, can I talk now?" It was only then that I realised she had not uttered a word from the time we had walked into the arms of the Soviet soldiers on the outskirts of the town.

When we reached the hotel, one of the porters recognised me and we – that is Ildi and I – were given a room with a private bathroom. I was putting her to bed when I heard a knock on the door. I was frightened, believing it was the Russians, but it turned out to be my friend the porter.

"Every room is being searched, but don't worry, I told them you are my sister" he said. I was lucky. The money I had given him on my arrival had obviously done its job. In cases like this it is better to tip 'before' and not 'after'.

The next morning we had to return to the Russian Headquarters to meet up with my colleagues of the night before, who included two distant cousins of mine. We were then ordered to go to the railway station to board the train for Budapest, but as we approached the station we met people on their way back.

"There's no point in going further – there's a strike and there are no trains running", they informed us. I was very relieved because the last thing I wanted was to go back to Budapest.

By this time I was desperate for a cup of coffee, so I suggested to the others that we should go and find a good cup of Espresso before deciding on our next move. We went into a little coffee shop and as we went in I noticed a woman sitting with her back towards the door. She was dressed in an expensive moss-green coat and an ocelot fur hat. I decided she must be from Budapest because people did not dress like that in the provinces.

Later, as I was sitting in my room with Ildi, I had an unexpected visitor. Unknown to me a friend of mine called Frank Klug had also been desperately trying to leave Hungary. He was a member of the Hungarian Opera House and had a wonderful tenor voice. I wasn't even aware that he wanted to escape that night but there he was standing at my door.

After we'd greeted each other he came in and asked me to tell him exactly what our movements had been that day. I told him all we had done – going to the railway station, being told about the strike, coming back to the hotel and all that I could remember.

"You are leaving something out", he said. I then remembered the part about going for coffee.

"Was there anyone else in the coffee shop?" he asked.

"Well, yes, there was a woman in a gorgeous green wool coat, she was also wearing an ocelot hat", I replied.

"Mady, you made a grave mistake. You talked with the owner of the café about being captured and having been sent back to the town in front of that woman in the green coat and ocelot hat".

Up until then he had been very straight faced. I had taken him seriously and was quite worried until he informed me, with a grin, that she was his wife and had listened to the conversation, but had wanted to remain incognito. After that conversation we all got together, and with the help of the owner of the café, who told us that her son and daughter were already in Vienna, having escaped earlier on, we 'contracted' another man to take us to the border.

The following morning eight or nine of us, accompanied by two very large Hungarians with an axe slung over their shoulders looking like a couple of mass murderers, walked through town towards the Austrian border. I really believed those men would chop us up, bury our bodies and steal all our money, but they didn't. Instead they took us as far as the 'no-man's land' and on the way they guided us beneath the guns of the Russian tanks. We paid them and they left us to our own devices. I had asked the others if anyone could speak German. They said, "Of course", but when the need arrived, no one could utter a word. I was the only one.

We walked through woods for hours in the rain. It became dark and we were soaked through to the skin, but we kept on walking until we eventually saw some village lights in the distance, and it was at that moment that Frank slipped and broke his leg. One of my cousins offered to stay with him until help arrived, and we left them with Frank singing 'La Donna E'mobile' from Verdi's Rigoletto, to keep awake.

We reached a village and I banged on the window of the first house we came across. A peasant woman came to the door, and I told her who we were and about Frank having broken his leg. Her husband and brother-in-law went back to pick up Frank with a stretcher made from two stepladders tied together and they brought him back to the house.

It had been a filthy night, pouring with rain. We had walked for fourteen hours before arriving at that Austrian village. It seemed as if they were prepared for us. The very kind Austrian woman gave us hot milk and bread.

"Can you tell me where we are – what is the name of this place?" I asked.

She hesitated, and after a moment she said "Do you see those lights over there, those are the lights of Sopron and they are only two and a half miles away, and this village is called Nickeldorf".

It had taken us all that time, sliding and slipping, walking backwards, forwards and sideways, and up and down in the mud and rain, only to cover a distance of two and a half miles. But we counted ourselves fortunate because some poor people had wandered back into Hungary in their confusion. There was no way of knowing where one was, and of course it was pitch black.

The woman's husband then directed us to a temporary camp in the village where we were taken in for the night and put to sleep on straw. Ildi slept on one side of me and on the other side was a friend of Mr. and Mrs Klug who was an opera producer I'd never met before that night. We all slept huddled together with my tenor friend and his wife nearby. When I opened my eyes in the morning I found a Hungarian bending over me, saying, "I hope you're not Jewish – you're not Jewish by any chance are you?"

"Of course not" responded the opera producer before I could say anything "What are you talking about, this is my wife and daughter. Anyway, why do you ask? What happens if someone is Jewish?"

"It's not important, only Jews don't get cocoa for breakfast" was the reply!

That was my first morning in Austria. It was after the war, after the Russian Occupation, and after the Hungarian Revolution, and that particular Hungarian still hadn't learned a thing. (And there were many more that did not either.) It was nice of the producer to pretend that we were a family. I never saw him again after that morning.

We had been lucky, because that day we were taken to a big camp in a town called Lichtenstein (not the country Lichtenstein), 30 or 35 kilometres from Vienna. Here we were placed in decent accommodation.

I started to go out with the ambulance; because being fluent in German they needed me as an interpreter. Someone was always willing to look after my daughter, Ildi, for me. We had heard that the famous film 'Gone with the Wind' was playing in a cinema in Vienna. We had all read the book and wanted to see the film for years, but although it was in Budapest in the Film Museum, the Communists would not show it. It was "too American", "too capitalistic", or "too Catholic"; the Russians were afraid of the "propaganda". A group of us went into the city with the intention of seeing it, but wandered into the American Embassy and asked if we could get on the quota. I had already had a telegram from Valy and her husband, refusing to send us papers to get into Sweden. They were afraid of us becoming burdens. It did hurt me, but I could not really blame them.

The film was going to play from the following Monday.

The Americans didn't want a divorced woman with a young child either. The Canadians had no quotas open at that time but were nice enough to advise us to go to the British Embassy, which was very near to the cinema, playing the film of our dreams. So my little group and I went over to see what the 'Brits' were going to say about letting us into Britain and to Canada. It was a Friday.

"I can't do anything for you today, our quota is full" we were told.

On the Monday we went back to Vienna to see 'Gone with the Wind' at last. As we were near to 'Stephan Kirche' (Stephan church), I said to the others, "let's see if the English have something for us".

Peter said, "They won't, we were here Friday". However, I was always a very determined person and said, "let's just try".

The nice lady recognised us, and asked how many we were. "Twelve" we replied.

She handed us twelve little pieces of numbered papers. They were not bigger, nor did they look more important than cloakroom tickets. We were told to be there the next morning at 9.30am, children, luggage and all. We missed the film again! However, I have since made up for it, watching the film several times.

The morning of the next day we were put into lovely comfortable coaches and started on our journey all the way to London.

There were three coaches, and in our coach the guides were a couple from the Hungarian aristocracy – count and Countess Esterhasy. By this time they had to work for their living because the Russians had confiscated all their estates, and they were only left with their titles, with nothing to live on.

Our first stop was in Ulm where we were accommodated in a really nice hotel. We had wonderful rooms and great food.

Our second stop, if I remember correctly, was in Cologne where we stayed in a Youth Hostel, not as wonderful as the hotel in Ulm, but we were compensated with a visit to the truly magnificent Cathedral. It was astonishing that during the war it had not been destroyed.

Our third stop was in Namur in Belgium.

The next stop was Lille.

The following day we were taken to the ferry in Calais, from where we reached the shores of our 'Promised Land', and in the same coach drove to London. Here we were taken to a really ugly place – it looked like a workhouse, left over from the 'Dickens' era. A policeman opened the gates and we were ushered into some barrack-looking building. Countess Esterhasy assured us that this was only for one night and we were not to worry.

The next day we were ushered back on to the coach and were once again on our way, but had no idea where. I should mention at this point that it was now 23rd December 1956, the day before Christmas Eve. It was cold and as we were driving towards the late afternoon, the countryside became bleak, very bleak and snowy. We did not see many cars, only some agricultural vehicles, and little else. I started to feel that we must have been going too far away from any civilisation. However, all of a sudden there was a house, a big house with lights on the outside. We stopped, a woman appeared on the doorstep wearing black corduroy trousers and a thick emerald green turtle neck sweater, hand knitted in 'fisherman's rib'. She said "Hello", and immediately took the hand of Ildi (the smallest child amongst the Hungarians), ushering her into the big house. The name of the house was New Field Hall. We were in Yorkshire, just outside Skipton – the address 'Bell Bask'.

I spoke no English, but I knew that a new life had just started for all of us.

CHAPTER TEN

~ Freedom – Cardiff, the Promised Land ~

New Field Hall was a beautiful big old house, used for holidays only. It was very cold. There was no central heating of course, just three open fires in the whole large building. They gave us all stone (clay) bed-warmers, which made our beds nice and comfortable.

The people looking after us were all volunteers, giving up their precious time for the Hungarian refugees. The woman in the emerald green sweater on the doorstep was a kind schoolteacher from Cardiff, her name Dorothy Whiston. There was also an interpreter – a Hungarian girl called Anne Beer who had lived in Toronto since the end of the war, but who was on a post graduate course in England. She had volunteered her Christmas holiday to help us. There was also an American from California called Vernon Faulkner.

We also had a very nice English lady who cooked all our meals. This lady had a female golden Labrador, very friendly; we all loved her. On Christmas Day our lovely cook produced a wonderful dinner for us, beautifully roasted turkey, with all the trimmings. We really enjoyed our dinner until we were served something that was hot and brown! We all tried to eat it but we couldn't. Because we didn't want to hurt her feelings, first we tried the dog. But instead of eating it she left the dining room, and then in desperation we tried to put it on the fire! Then the fire went out! There was nothing left for us to do, but to very apologetically take what was obviously our first Christmas pudding back to the kitchen. Since then I have learned to love it!

During our three-week stay in Yorkshire, people living in the neighbourhood heard that among the Hungarian refugees was a 26-year-old divorced woman with a small child. The belief was that all Hungarians were good cooks, so I – with the help of our interpreter – started to get offers for jobs as a cook or housekeeper. I would not have minded taking a job in a household, thinking that would give us a home, and living with British people would also mean that I would be able to learn English quickly. However, the schoolteacher from Cardiff, Dot, was very put out by these offers; she obviously did not want me to become a housekeeper and invited my daughter and me to go to Cardiff for a few weeks. In Cardiff I would be able to look around to see what I might do to make a living.

However, before we even arrived in Cardiff, Dot had tried to speak with one of the Rabbis about me and asked if there was any help they could give us. Dot did tell him – when eventually he came to the phone – all there was to tell, that I was a survivor of the Camps; and that I was there with a small child; etc., etc.

Dot was told that I should not worry, someone would call me very soon, from – if I remember correctly – a glove factory, where I would get a job. Neither Dot nor I worried, and I am glad that we didn't, because we could still be worrying! You see we have never heard a word from the rabbi or anyone else for that matter!

I knew that I would be totally on my own, with the exception of my newly found friend Dot.

Some time went by before I started to realise the possible reason for the fact that they not only totally ignored us, but also avoided any contact with us. This was the time when 'we' were still an awkward kind of subject. Nobody really knew what – if anything – to do with us. I am still wondering if it had something to do with a kind of guilt. Not only were we in the Camps while they were fortunate enough to live in the security of this country, but that now, on top of everything else, we appeared in Great Britain, maybe upsetting the peace by just being there.

It still puzzles me though, because there were very few of us who were refugees for the second time - the first time out of the hell of Hitler's camps, and now out of the communist hell of Stalin and what came after him.

Dot had never seen me before and certainly didn't know me, and although she only had a one-bedroom flat she moved out of her bedroom and gave it to Ildi and me. I was also fortunate enough to have been given a cot for Ildi by a Roman Catholic priest in Yorkshire.

I have mentioned my two distant cousins before. Peter, at the time we came to Britain, was 19 years old. He was an excellent student in 'gimnasium' and wanted to go to university to study to become a stage producer. My beautiful old friend, the by this time very famous actor Lajos Basti (remember, his father returned from France in the summer of 1946), was the head of the committee who examined young people wanting to go on the stage. He told Peter, with great sorrow, that there was no 'space' for producers, but that he could go to train to become an actor. I have just asked Peter if I remembered all this correctly, and he pointed out that I had left out one important detail: they had asked him if he could sing. He did not want to show up Tito Gobi, so he did not sing for them. He became a printer in his dad's printing works and, immediately upon his arrival in Cardiff, got a job.

His younger brother, Andras was 16 years old. He continued his high school studies in Cathays High School in Cardiff and later became an engineer. Both of them married British girls.

On our arrival in Cardiff I had £6 in cash. It was my only fortune. A few days later Dot took me to David Morgan department store where, using Dot's name, I purchased a knitting machine, putting down £5.00 and the rest on 'Hire Purchase'. I made a red cable stitch cardigan with some of the wool I had received from the nice people of Yorkshire, who believed that all Hungarian women must be good knitters, and they bought 35lbs of beautiful wool into Newfield Hall. I was lucky because I was the only one who knitted! This was a natural present from them, because Yorkshire at that time was still wool country.

The red cable stitch cardigan was made for Dot's sister, Cora, who was also a schoolteacher. When she wore the cardigan for the first time she came home from school with 8 orders for my cable stitch cardigan! I was in business!

I had a lot of orders for my sweaters and cardigans, because luckily for me it was the time before mass imports started, and because I made very beautiful, made-to-measure garments I managed to earn a living. I worked hard day and night.

The National Assistance Board gave me £4 and some shillings a week to live on, because they didn't want me to go out to work and leave my daughter at home. I started to work hard and eventually took my National Assistance chequebook back, because I didn't want to take their money any more. Mr. Thomas, who was the officer who looked after me, asked me several times if I was sure that I could manage without my National Assistance, and I insisted that I could. However before he took my book he asked me to sit down for a minute, and disappeared into a back office.

All of a sudden all the people from the offices came into the front office where I was sitting to have a look at me, then without saying a word, they went back to their desks. I was then told that I was the first person in the history of that office to have voluntarily relinquished the chequebook!

I still go into David Morgan's store regularly and sometimes wander into the knitting machine department, where back in 1957 I purchased my first knitting machine. I remember my visits to this department where all kinds of yarns were displayed in beautiful colours. I used to stand there for hours just watching women pick some wool or cotton, just pay for it and leave with it in a bag.

This brought back memories of our knitting time in Communist Hungary, where we knitted for our 'Collective' or 'Co-operative', making sweaters for Soviet export. We were given wool, out of which we had to knit both plain backs and sleeves or fancy fronts. When one was 'on the plain bits' we had to produce 24 – 36 bits (a sleeve or a back was a 'bit') in order to earn a little money. We had to deliver once a week. The evening before, we took the knitted pieces down to the cellar to make them a little damp, so when it was weighed in the next day, we managed to 'steal' maybe an ounce of wool. Every month or so we had a meeting and tried to swap our little balls of wool and after a few months all of us (friends) could make up a sweater with a bit of luck. The Soviet system made thieves out of us because of the miserable monies they paid for our hard work.

So you get the picture of my being in a state of unbelievable daydreaming, watching women being able to just buy wool, not having to connive and steal, just choose it and pay for it. How wonderful this newly found freedom was. I did not have to worry about a possible jail sentence for buying wool that was smuggled into the country either.

By the time I arrived in Cardiff, about five weeks after leaving Hungary, Marta's little Kathy no longer existed. She had died as a result of the neglect caused by the fighting and injuries to the crowds outside the hospital in Budapest.

For the ten years I had lived in Communist Hungary I could do nothing to help my former teacher Gabriella Kovesi, but I did little things for her when I lived in Britain, and after I'd started making a meagre living for my daughter and myself. I sent her Christmas parcels and I remember once sending her a second-hand sheepskin coat – couldn't afford a new one – and she wrote telling me that in her wildest dreams she could not imagine owning a 'fur coat'. I visited her each time I went to Hungary and she told me on my first visit:

"Mady, my forty five years in the teaching profession have all been made worthwhile by having one pupil like you".

I felt then and I feel today that it was one of the most wonderful compliments I was ever given in my life. How totally desperate I must have been to feel so good about her actually wanting me to return. But she did want to see me again – I did return, didn't I?

Living in Cardiff was probably the easiest period of my life. Because we had fewer demands on life, our every day achievement gave us satisfaction; temptations were smaller, so life was easier.

My daughter went to nursery school straight after our arrival. It was beautifully arranged with Dot's help. The head teacher, Mrs. Smith even purchased an English-Hungarian dictionary to help them communicate with Ildi. They never needed to use it, because being 3 ½ years old she picked English up in days. I remember walking home with her from school one afternoon. I was talking to her in Hungarian and she answered me in English! This, I thought is my cue to hurry up and learn the new language as quickly as possible!

This time I already did the grocery shopping by myself. I had even learned to work out the very complicated British money. Dot did not accept any rent from me, so I reciprocated by shopping and cooking for the three of us. I am a born cook; it was easy for me to 'take over' the kitchen!

Going to Clifton Street for cabbages and meat and all the other things we needed, and trying to communicate with the grocer, the butcher and the baker helped me to pick up English, which in time became my favourite language. Dot, being a schoolteacher, helped me a lot. She made me read The Observer on Sundays and it was not so terribly long before I more or less understood some of the articles I had read. The radio was a great help too. The BBC played an important part in my learning of this great language.

During the early spring of 1957, only a few months after my arrival in Cardiff, I managed to read – and understand (more or less) – an article in the paper of the last interview with Humphrey Bogart, who was terminally ill with cancer. I remember reading something like…."Cancer is the only really democratic thing, because it does not make any difference if you are tall, short, ugly, beautiful, rich or poor, it will take you…" How right he was.

Of course, speaking German made it easier too. Learning English from Hungarian must have been very difficult, since Hungarian, which belongs to the 'Fin-Ugor' language family, has nothing in common with English, with the exception of a few words with Latin origin.

When Peter, some friends and I first went to Stratford upon Avon, we had tickets to see Shakespeare's Julius Caesar. We must have felt brave, and I do remember thinking that it was lucky that we knew the story, because we could not understand the old English yet!

A funny story comes into my mind about Hungarians and the new language. I had some people around for coffee – it might have been dinner – and among them a newly wed couple, a very nice British lady doctor and her husband, a Hungarian refugee medical student. It was obvious that he married her to be able to go through medical school with her financing him.

We were talking about the 'old country' – it was early on – and the name of Janos Arany came into the conversation. Mr. Arany was a Hungarian poet of some stature, who was an early admirer of Shakespeare - he was born around 1817 - and translated many of the Bard's works beautifully. What made this very interesting was that Mr. Arany did not speak English!

Well, the young Hungarian – whose name I cannot remember, which is just as well as he would get upset if he was to read this – if indeed anyone will ever read this –suddenly said he is "sending his wife to Hungary for six months to learn Hungarian"!

We all asked, "What on earth for, it is totally useless once you stepped over the border."

His answer was surprising, to say the least: "I want her to be able to read Shakespeare in Arany's translation…"

We were ever so happy – and proud – to be able to read it in its original language. He obviously was one of the people who did not want to assimilate into the life of our adopted country.

I've written 'adopted' country – should I not have written 'adopting' country? After all, this country adopted us. We had no difficulties in becoming British, no one ever called us foreigners, and the problem of 'political asylum' did not exist for us.

The Hungarian writer George Mikes wrote in his book 'How to be an Alien', that when a British person starts to talk, from his accent others can tell not only which part of the country he came from, but in most cases what type of education he or she received. Posh or not! We, 'aliens' have our accent, which very successfully disguises where we came from and if we went to a decent school.

One of the biggest dreams in my life was to go to Florence. I had seen books, pictures, saw some of the town in films and knew that I needed to go there. So, in the summer of 1958 – before I had a British passport – with a 'Travel Document' I ventured out of South Wales and, by train of course, went to Florence with a large group of people.

These organised trips were in Embryo State, but it all worked out well. I fulfilled my dream and saw as much as I possibly could. The Gallery Uffici was, of course, the biggest sensation, because so many of the paintings I had learned about in school were there 'in the flesh'.

The Ponte Vecchio was unbelievable with those little shops, and the fantastic jewellery, fabulous leather things, beautiful fashion items; Florence made a great impression, with its art and the beauty of the town itself. And, of course, the food! The wonderful Italian food! I fell in love and I still am in love with Florence.

Travelling once a year to 'the Continent' became a routine. Ildi and I went to Paris and Italy several times, Sweden, and from 1964 on Canada and the United States and back to Hungary.

CHAPTER ELEVEN

~ Integration ~

During this time I bought my first house, a Victorian terraced house in a nice part of Cardiff, with the benefit of a 100% mortgage, since I had no money. Mr. Macmillan was the Prime Minister and offered 100% mortgages to people who were willing to buy old houses. My God, I was British and I was buying my own house!

It was our first home and we loved it. The house had three bedrooms and a 'box room', and I managed to have 'lodgers' in order to make extra money. The 'boys', Peter and Andras, who came with us to Britain in 1956, moved in and I even cooked for them!

I don't think I made a great deal of profit because I could not charge them a lot, and also because I always bought good ingredients with which to make good meals!

My little 'business' was going well, I was working very long hours, but I worked in the house and saved time most people spend commuting. Nice people ordered cardigans, sweaters, etc., and I made them with pleasure.

Around 1959 I was brave enough to open a tiny shop in Cardiff in the Castle Arcade. I had an even tinier workroom upstairs. I sold knitwear, all made by me, and a little later started to 'buy in' hand made 'things', all from Central (and East) Europe.

In the little shop I started to have a regular customer: an old lady who wore a long brown Harris Tweed cape, and a brown felt hat – she had snow white hair piled upon her head and into the hat. She walked with the help of a cane. She came to see me – and bought some things – every week, and I found out from her that she was a retired schoolteacher.

When spring came, the old lady started to wear a beige Harris Tweed cape, a beige straw hat – same shape as the brown felt hat was in the winter. She started to order very unusual things, like pink fine wool machine-knitted nightdresses, always with a yoke and a little 'Peter Pan' collar. I had to do tiny fine embroidery on the yoke and the collar. These nightdresses were more expensive than the little handmade things she used to buy before and I always made sure that I gave her a 10-15% discount. After all, I knew that schoolteachers were not overpaid in this country either.

One day Mr. Grey, the secretary of the Manager – a famous man in Cardiff, Arthur McTaggarth Short – of the Arcade, came down to see me and said:

"Mady, I haven't seem Miss Howell lately, has she been in?"

"Who is Miss Howell?" I asked.

"Don't you know that the elderly lady in the cape is Miss Mabel Howell?" he replied.

I did not know that my retired school teacher who was my – by this time – much liked and respected customer – actually was one of the daughters of Mr. James Howell, who not only built Howell's Department Store, but also the beautiful Park Hotel, and lots more everlasting establishments in Cardiff!

Miss Howell became a friend, of whose friendship I was very proud. I still am. She told me that she was one of the first female science students in, I think, Oxford – but I don't remember, it might have been Cambridge. She had to go to lectures with a chaperone – how times have changed!

Miss Howell was the same age as Sir Winston Churchill. I have learned a lot from Miss Howell, who was an extremely wise lady. I was complaining to her once that I was still 'at my age' – I was 29 or 30 at this time – very bad in judging people. (I still believe everything people tell me and get hurt by some people taking advantage of my stupidity).

I was talking about a partner I had in the little shop who had left me with debts I had to pay back. Miss Howell said to me that I am still better off than those people, who are suspicious of everyone, because even if I get hurt sometimes, most of the time I enjoy people, friendships, etc. Suspicious people don't enjoy anyone, or anything, ever.

Miss Howell loved Ildi too, although totally against 'people sleeping together' – she was a spinster, of course – I could never talk about actually being married in order to have my daughter. She lived in Park Place, her windows overlooking the Park at the Civic Centre. She used to stand in her window and get upset when 'young people disappeared together'. "Can you imagine, dear, what they are up to?" she asked several times. When I mentioned that I also had to 'do something' to get Ildi, she said, with great dignity and knowledge, "that is different dear".

From this statement I realised that Miss Howell liked me!

I was quite busy most of the time and was dreaming about having somebody to help me. I had no idea how or where I could find the person who could work with me and who would be interested in taking a job in a mini sized business, for the money I could afford to pay. One morning, it was a very cold morning; I noticed that a very beautiful Chinese girl was walking up and down the Arcade. I called her into my warm shop, and she told me that her boss was late; he was driving in from Swansea, a Mr. Lewis who had the knitting machine shop in the Arcade. We started to talk. I must have told her that I was looking for a co-worker; for she told me that her sister Lily might be interested in the job. Sure enough, the next day, Lily arrived. We started not only to work together, but at that time, unbeknown to us both, we also started a life-long friendship. Lily was a graduate of Cardiff Art College. She was – and is – a great dressmaker and a very special human being.

Some years later 'we' moved into a slightly bigger shop in Wellfield Road, at the Roath Park. We started to pick up some wonderful customers, some becoming friends. We did many things, dressmaking, machine knitting, made-to-measure and for stock.

We worked well together and enjoyed our work, building up a reputation for good quality, good prices, nice styles and always beautiful colours. Now, 40-ish years later we still hear sometimes that we were the only ones who were willing – and able – to make something out of a small piece of fabric.

In the late 90's I met two ex-customers who told me that in the early 60's when businessmen started to travel to Hong Kong, and other parts of the Orient, they both received small pieces of silk. They went all over Cardiff, but no one would take the pieces, everyone said they were too small to make anything out of them. They came to us, and not only did we make a dress each for the two ladies, but also a little jacket! I loved the story; it was so nice of them to remember.

One of these ladies also told me – in the middle 90's – that she still had the last knitted dress and jacket that we made for her. She said that they had been invited to a posh wedding and she needed a special outfit. Her husband had suggested that she came back to us. We had agreed on a colour and style, but then she said she had to ask her husband before she gave us the order because it was going to be 'very dear'. I asked her how much had we charged her. She said "Ten guineas"!

Her husband had said, “It is a lot of money, but Mady always makes you such nice things”!

As I was starting to be ‘known’, some of our customers used to come in for a cup of tea and a chat. One of these ladies was a Mrs. Nancy Summers, who had invited me to their magnificent house on Cyn Coed Road, for dinner on a few occasions. Mrs. Summers and her husband Morlais Summers learned about my ‘past’ from me during one of these dinners.

One day Mrs Summers came into the shop and asked if I would make a donation to one of her charities, supporting ‘Christian Aid’. I said I would.

Mrs. Summers said “Mady dear, you are such a wonderful Christian”.

I said “but, Mrs. Summers….” She said “that makes no difference, dear”.

This must have been around the time that my daughter, Ildi, was ready to go to religious instruction classes. I phoned the secretary of the Synagogue to ask if Ildi could go to Sunday school.

He said “Well, yes, but of course, before that you have to become a member of the congregation”.

After I said that was OK, he told me the amount that I would have to pay for a membership fee. Since I didn’t earn that much money, I said my thanks and stated that I could not afford that sort of money. I was not offered a smaller fee.

I remember explaining to Ildi that I decided to let her grow up without religious education and when she was old enough she would be able to decide for herself.

This must have been a decision I gave a lot of thought to. I felt then (and I have felt ever since) that religion – all kind of religions – has caused a lot of tragedy for a great number of people, and while I respect everybody’s religion, for me my own beliefs work only. That maybe if people were allowed to form their own religion and live a decent life, be good to others, learn about the religions of others, try to understand human behaviour; try to help whenever and wherever they can, maybe there would be less hatred in the world.

Maybe also there would be not so many people who are always ready and willing to kill, to hurt, cheat, and all the other terrible things people do to each other.

So, I think at that time my life had changed. I started to believe that it does not matter what your own religion is, it does not make any difference whose church you are standing in. What does matter is only how you behave toward others. Maybe I had started to believe in this long before, only I was not quite so clear about it.

This also was about the time when some interesting things happened to me. One of these was that the head of the 'Alien Department' of the Cardiff Police asked me if I was interested in becoming the 'official' interpreter in Court!

My English was obviously good enough for him to feel that I could do the job, and I – of course – accepted with great anticipation. I have served during several cases, some of which were dangerous enough to warrant a policeman to stand on either side of me during the session. Some of my 'clients' were only thieves, but one or two of them were more serious criminals. These were the Hungarians who perhaps were set free, when during the revolution in '56, the prisons were opened and they were all released.

Another great thing that made a difference to us – Lily and I – was that the Wardrobe mistresses of the BBC TV Wales presented us with a three-year contract, which was wonderful.

We made outfits and costumes for TV plays and programmes. Some famous actresses came for fittings and that was really exciting for us!

Ildi was going to the Marlborough Road School and I had my first car. It was of course a Morris 1000, 'Forest green' with a soft-top. It was lovely but old and sometimes we used cellotape to 'repair' the roof, but we loved it. The registration number plate read: ROT 533!

In around 1963, I think, Adolph Eichmann was captured by the Israelis in South America. All the memories came back after all those years. I was as interested in the case as anyone could have been who has actually met this totally cruel monster of a man.

To my great surprise someone called me from the Welsh BBC TV and asked me if I would be willing to be interviewed on television about Herr Eichmann. I did it; I obviously used my own experiences and my own feelings about a man whose cruelty was so complete. I, of course remembered those sad concerts in Auschwitz, with a slogan in big letters at the gates ***"ARBEIT MACHTS FREI"*** – "WORK MAKES FREE". When the Germans knew that the war was lost – in 1944 – Herr Eichmann was still determined to finish the 'problem of the Hungarian Jews'. I was in the studio and talked about some of the things that had happened to me when I was 14 years old, not knowing whether I would survive or just go after all the others. Now, some 19 years later, here I was living in a great country with my daughter, in security, in the house I was buying, and wearing nice clothes. And I even spoke good enough English to be interviewed by the same BBC that gave us the only hope we had before our deportation.

This was also the same BBC which kept us informed over the radio, and for which we risked our 'freedom' during the dark days of the Stalin regime, too. I was honoured to be asked, and if the subject had been a different one, I would have been happy to do it. This way, I did it not only because they picked me out from all the Hungarians living in South Wales, but also because I thought it important to keep the subject of the holocaust alive.

It was quite horrific to watch the trial of Eichmann on the television – we had a small black & white set by this time.

During the whole time he did not show the slightest regret, not a twitch of his face gave you the feeling that after all those years maybe, just maybe he would say a quick "sorry". He was convinced that he was right. He was a great soldier and a loyal servant of the 'other Adolf'.

Listening to the radio – which I did a lot – opened up a whole new world to me about all the things people in the West have enjoyed for years, but we in the Soviet world were not allowed to know about. One of those things was American – and British – light music and the people who provided it. We knew about George Gershwin, and Glenn Miller, but precious little else. I had received a 78 record of Gershwin's Rhapsody in Blue as a wedding present in 1952. You can imagine being as poor we were that this was a big present. In Cardiff I started to listen to the magic of Satchmo, Ella Fitzgerald, Nat King Cole and the others, and while I was already a lover of opera, this kind of light music was very enjoyable. It was a natural thing therefore for Lily, her sister June and me to go to hear Nat King Cole in the Capitol Cinema, next door to the 'New Continental' Restaurant. Nat King Cole did not only sound wonderful; he also moved and looked wonderful. He was the first black star I saw on stage and I fell in love with him. My love lasted until the day he died and forever after.

This was also the first time we were entertained by the incomparable Victor Borge. I was lucky not only to be able to understand him in my new language, but to understand his wonderful sense of humour as well.

I started to go to the theatre to see operas, my biggest joy, in my spare time. The little theatre in the town was a favourite with thousands of people and it certainly became mine. We were lucky to see some of the best classics, both in plays and operas. The Welsh Opera Company was great and the singers, not only the soloists, but also members of the chorus were wonderful. I knew when I first went that Welsh men are great singers. All you had to do those days was to pass a pub on any evening to listen to the men drinking their beer and singing!

One of the most beautiful of Verdi's operas: 'Nabucco' was performed during my Cardiff life and I saw it and never forgot it. Very few companies can perform it – so I learned later on – because of the size of the chorus. The Welsh chorus was exquisite; I loved every minute of it.

I saw Olivier, Michael Redgrave and other great stage artists in many wonderful plays. I went to see David Kossoff's 'One man show', which he did about the time his 'rewrite' of the Bible was published. It was modern, easy to read and also to understand, and one could enjoy it regardless of one's religion. I thought at the time that if they would teach religion in that style, more people would follow it.

We – a few of us – were so keen to take in what the British stage offered, that we sometimes took the train to London to see a matinee. One of these trips was to see Turgener's 'Month in the Country'. Starring Ingrid Bergman and Michael Redgrave. When the curtain went up everyone stopped breathing. What a gorgeous sight! Miss Bergman wearing a fabulous period summer dress, reclining on a Victorian chaise longue. The play was out of this world, of course – never to be forgotten.

After the show – and before going back to Paddington Station, we – as it became customary – went to Soho, where in Old Compton Street, a certain Madame Floris had two shops opposite each other. The one was a small coffee shop with tables and chairs, selling good coffee and the famous Floris pastries and cakes, the other one selling her handmade chocolate.

Let me tell you a little bit about Madame Maria Floris. She was the daughter of Mr. Floris of Budapest. He had a very well known confectioner's shop and made really fantastic cakes and pastries. Madame Floris came to Britain, I think just before the war and became a very famous patissierer in London. She rose to such heights in her profession, that later on she was commissioned by Lady Churchill to make Sir Winston's birthday cakes. She also made some birthday and wedding cakes for the noble and aristocratic families, and I think, even for some members of the Royal Family.

Somebody introduced me to Madame Floris early on. On the afternoon of watching Miss Bergman and Mr. Redgrave on stage, we went for our coffee and perhaps even a piece of cake (or was it two pieces?)

We sat at a table near to the door, and Madame Floris came in, looking every bit of the regal, stunning, very tall and upright lady that she was. She was wearing a long black Victorian dress, with a fitted bodice, tight around the waist and with a full skirt. It was buttoned all the way to the neck with tiny jet buttons and a high neck. (She must have made a terrific impression upon me, because now, some 40 years later I can still see her).

She had on a necklace, the likes of which I have never seen before or since. The necklace was made out of small, oval shape pieces of gold, covered with 'cobalt' enamel, and in the centre of each piece was a tiny flower made out of pearls, with ruby insides and tiny leaves made out of emeralds. The large pendant was the same, only twenty times larger than the small pieces. It was long – she was tall – and it came down well below her bust. My eyes must have left their sockets staring, because she turned to me and said: "Oh, I remember you. You are the girl from Cardiff; I notice you like my chain".

I told her that I had never seen anything like it and asked if it was made by Faberge?

She replied that it was, and did I want to hear the story of it? Of course I said yes, so here it is:

The necklace indeed was made by the most famous Russian jewellery maker: Peter Carl Faberge. He made the most beautiful objects, not only jewellery, but also boxes and other ornaments. One of his most famous pieces was the jewelled Easter Egg. He used precious and semi-precious stones only.

Well, the necklace of Madame Floris was, in fact given to her father by the last Russian Czar, Nicholas. He was shot with his family by the Soviets, in 1918. The Czar must have been happy with the cakes Mr Floris made him too.

As a footnote: Mr. Faberge lost his business too; it was destroyed by the Communists, and he died in exile in Switzerland in 1920.

By the way, Madame Floris offered to let me try the necklace on. I haven't been the same since…

CHAPTER TWELVE

~ Journeys around the world ~

In the summer of 1963 I took Ildi to Sweden for a two-week holiday. We were going to spend one week in beautiful 'Varmland', which is the Lake District of Sweden. We were invited by the mother of Christine, the lovely Swedish Au Pair, who had looked after Ildi the year before. Karin, the mother was – and still is – a stunning Swedish blonde, then already divorced, with three children: Christine, Carl Johan and Elizabeth, the youngest, who was ten years old, the same as Ildi. They gave us a wonderful time. Karin drove us over to Norway – what a beautiful country – she drove us to the Swedish 'West Coast' where people live on little islands and live outdoors from the minute the snow melts and the sun is warm. We stayed with Karin's best friend and her husband. They were all wonderful and the trip was unforgettable.

There was one little thing that surprised me: Swedes swam in the nude, regardless of who was around. I knew that they were totally uninhibited, but was not prepared for this. I already knew the saying "When in Rome, do as the Romans do", but I continued to swim in my swimsuit!

The little lakes in 'Varmland' are all over; you drive a bit, there is a lake; you get out for a swim, drive a little more, get out at another lake again.... The place is quite wonderful and we had a great time. (Karin has visited me here twice and I have visited her once since 1963. She is still beautiful).

After the super week in Karlstad, we took the train to Stockholm, where we were to visit Vally and her husband.

Lipot was a successful fur trader; I was surprised to see how inconvenient their apartment was. They lived on the third floor and although it was very nice the building was in the old part of town and there were no lifts – everything had to be carried up three flights of stairs.

"Why do you live in this building where there are no lifts? It must be very difficult carrying everything up and down the stairs," I said.

"Lipot has to be within walking distance of the Synagogue," said Vally. "Religious Jews are not permitted to ride in any vehicle on the Sabbath".

Whilst we were there I wasn't allowed to touch anything in the kitchen for fear of contaminating the food – milk and meat products and their respective dishes, cloths, tea towels and cooking utensils had to be kept separate. I almost caused chaos on my first day with them but soon realised what the rules were. I had never been subjected to this kind of regime during my upbringing – it was totally alien to me. Imagine my surprise when Friday afternoon came and the usual toilet roll was removed to be replaced by cutout paper squares that were pushed on to a hook on the wall. It was forbidden to tear paper on the Sabbath – lifting it off the hook was acceptable but tearing it was not.

Lippi's preparation for the Friday evening service in the synagogue was something to behold. First he took off his suit and put on a better one with Vally making sure that there was nothing left in his pockets. Then he put a handkerchief inside the belt of his trousers with a small comb folded into the handkerchief – they explained to me that you were allowed to wear things but not carry them. Wearing isn't work but carrying is and on Saturdays and Holy days you are not permitted to do any work. Even the light switch in the flat had to be operated by the Janitor who came up to switch it on and off along with the electric or gas cooker to heat up food. I wondered then and I still wonder what difference that sort of thing makes to being a religious person. In any case, when these laws were written there were no cars and no electric cookers.

Vally and Lippi lived together for about thirty years until Vally's death from cancer. During that time she never ever found out a thing about Lippi's five children. She never knew what sex they were, what ages they were, what their names were even, because he could never talk about them. That loving, caring, deeply religious man was so destroyed by what had happened to him that he could not discuss the details – not even with Vally. He must have been hurting terribly, especially as he wasn't able to share his grief. Some time later I learned that he had moved to Israel, where he quietly passed away.

During our few days stay in Stockholm I managed to meet my old boss from the Ministry of Planning, for whom I worked, back in the dark years of Stalinism. His name is John (Janos) Vago and he is what the Swedes call a 'diploma Injenior'. He is about 86 years old now and blessed with not only 'all his marbles', but with an excellent sense of humour and beautiful handwriting. He took us up to one of the hills overlooking the magnificent city of Stockholm, also known as the 'Venice of the North'. On this hill they have a place, a unique place called 'Karl Milles Gardens'. Karl Milles was a Swedish sculptor specialising in elongated, stylised figures of young females and males, and all of them were made into fountains. After he died the Swedish art lovers, or the Government, purchased back – or at least tried to – Milles's work to put it all into this magnificent garden, dedicated to his artistry. This was a wonderful experience, and to this day I am grateful to Janos for taking us there.

We had a coffee – of course – together, during which I asked him what we were distributing during those years in the Ministry. He said: "Didn't you know - nothing!"

We were pushing piles of papers from one building to another. We made plans. After all, we were the important 'Ministry of Planning'!

He told Ildi that when I was his secretary (poor Janos!), he came to my desk, which was in one of the corners of his office, and asked nicely: "Mady dear, could you type this letter for me?"

I said "Don't bother me now, I will drop a stitch…!"

According to Janos, not only was I knitting under my desk, but also had organised the other girls too and soon all the secretaries and typists were knitting! Well, as I said, there were 2 – 3 people employed to do the job of one, and that was totally ridiculous!

In 1964 I took my daughter to Toronto for a few days and from there on to New York to see the World's Fair. We didn't have too much money and when my friend, Clara, arranged for us to stay with her cousin John, I welcomed the opportunity. Little did I know that poor John, who had been living in New York since 1947-48, was a very poor man indeed.

He was a little guy, a simple man who had a big heart. He could not put us up, but managed to arrange for us to have the apartment of his best friend. This friend was on holiday with his family; they went to stay in the mountains, called the Catskills. This was a famous place in New York State, not too far by car, very suitable for whole families to go to for a few weeks rest. The summers in the city were unbearably hot and humid, but in the mountains, much cooler. Hundreds – thousands – of mainly Jewish husbands took their wives and children up there at the beginning of the summer school holidays, dropped them off, went back to the city and visited them on week ends.

If you have seen the film 'Seven Year Itch', with gorgeous Marilyn Monroe, you got the picture. There were many hotels with swimming pools, tennis courts, and evening entertainment often with well-known stars.

Many stories, anecdotes and jokes originated in those mountains over the decades. One of the more famous stand-up comics, Jack Carter told the story, that when he got his first job in the Catskills; he was not sure how to drive up there. But he soon found the right highway, because the centre of the road was marked out with a wide white line, which was painted with soured cream! This was funny for people who have experienced the most important sensation offered by the hotels to their guests: Food! Food in huge quantities, from morning until almost the next morning!

Let me explain: Breakfast was a buffet with every conceivable food on display with the exception of meats. There was an assortment of cereals, Danish cakes of every description, plus other types of cakes, cheeses, soured cream, butter, breads, fruits -–you name it, it was available!

People ate breakfast for an hour or two; many little old ladies walked away with a few little items wrapped in paper napkins. I couldn't figure out when they had a chance to eat these, because lunch started at mid-day!

Many people were already standing in lines, and could hardly wait to eat again!

Lunch consisted again of a large selection of cooked food, in unbelievable piles, and even bigger dinners commenced from 7pm to 11pm!

After the evening show, or the endless card games, at around 11-11.30pm, 'midnight snacks' were put on tables, and to my total surprise, many people managed to 'put down a little snack' just to make sure they didn't get hungry during the night!

This eating pattern was very strange for me to understand during my only visit to the Catskills. I hated the place and therefore never repeated the visit.

But, back to poor John. His friend's name was Mr. Bacall and he was manufacturing men's hats. So Mr. and Mrs. Bacall and the young Bacalls' left the keys to their apartment with poor John and we – Ildi and I – moved in for the 6-7 days we were to spend in New York.

The apartment was nice enough – it was in one of those old buildings on the West Side of Manhattan, off the famous Broadway. All we needed was a clean bedroom and a clean bathroom. We had both. During the first few nights we could not enjoy the nice bedroom because the police and ambulance sirens kept us awake. Police sirens are not pleasant in any town, but in New York City they are awful. They are very loud, they shriek and as one siren stops, the next one starts. It was difficult to get used to, but after two nights we were so very tired we fell asleep!

Poor John was really very kind to us; he took us to the World's Fair and we talked for hours; he bought us food and sweets for Ildi. During our conversations I noticed that whatever we said, he quickly answered: "Tat is noting" – (this is not a spelling mistake, but many Hungarians cannot pronounce 'th's' – it comes out as a straight 'T'). He had it bigger, or better, whatever the subject would be.

The late and great Victor Borge said on one of his "One Man Shows': "It is difficult to pronounce 'th's', especially when they are next to each other!"

It took me a few days to realise that John was a labourer in a factory, making heavy steel doors for safety deposit cabinets for the strong rooms in banks. The work must have been very hard, physical work for a very small middle-aged man. He took us to see his 'home', and I never got over my shock when we were taken to a 'rooming house' also on the West-side of Manhattan, next to Broadway. The landlady owned the whole floor – or maybe several floors – and rented what we call 'bedsitting rooms' to people like John.

Ildi and I started to call him 'poor John' and we referred to him by that name until he died many years later.

I must add here two things about 'poor John': the first one is that I found out only later, much later, that my lovely friend Clara had got me together with him in order to 'fix me up' with him! What made her do that was that she – and her family – were convinced that like all Hungarians living in New York, John must be a millionaire! This was the result of letters, some 'care packages' the ex-pats sent back to the 'Old Country', always boasting about their success, the money they were making, etc., etc.!

The other thing about poor John was that when years later I moved into my very nice apartment in Manhattan, it took me a long time to have the courage to invite him to my home. He was living for twenty-something years in the same rooming house, and I took an apartment on the East Side in a reasonably high-class building. I had terrible guilt feelings about it.

I had met a few old friends from Kispest; they were all in small businesses, all working terribly hard. Real hard work was needed in New York in order to survive. The streets, against all propaganda were not paved with dollar bills. There was an old saying 'back home' in Hungary: "He (she) has found America"; this means "All is wonderful in the land of opportunities"; easy money, easy life. I am afraid many who believed that were very disappointed and many actually went back to Hungary, where it was easier to exist. And of course for many the language was a big problem.

Most of these old friends, who had spent eight years in New York by this time, spoke in a very strange manner. They had great difficulties not only with "th's" (as I have said before), but also the "w", which came out as a "v". It sounded like "I vent to vork and valked home aftervards".

They also created a 'new language'. It was a mixture of 'anglofied' Hungarian words, mixed with English words, which were converted into some strange lingo. One thing was clear to me then and is still clear now; I am forever grateful for not learning English in Brooklyn! Cardiff was much better. I still have – and always will – have an accent, but my English is very good and I love this language. I am careful not to make mistakes and am very upset if British born (and educated in Britain) people make them. Whenever someone speaks bad English, I always feel that they are abusing this beautiful language.

Anyway, back to the Hungarians in New York. Most of them lived within a Hungarian community. There was – and still is – a Catholic Church with a Hungarian priest. There was also a cultural centre where only Hungarians entertained – a club where only Hungarians played cards, and Hungarian restaurants; also a cinema where they were showing Hungarian films only. Of course, they all talked to each other in the lingo of the 'Old Country'. My question was: What is the point of living in a new Country if they speak, eat, listen to, read, or in other words do everything exactly as they did 'back home'?

Some things were different, though. They enjoyed freedom and they earned money if they worked. One or two of them were already successful after such a short time. They were all telling me that it was nice to see me but what am I doing in the 'fog' of England? I should be there in the 'Big Apple'!

The trip was exciting, we saw a lot, and the World's Fair was fantastic.

The first time we were allowed back into Hungary after our illegal departure was in the year of 1964. The Communists did not want us back – we were labelled as 'politically undesirable'. They must have become desperate because all of a sudden they gave us unconditional amnesty. Of course the natural tourist is the 'expat' who will go back to the old country and spend hard currency, which the country needs very badly.

Our first visit back was very interesting. After eight years in Britain it was sad to see how terribly run down and poor looking Budapest was. We were walking in the beautiful Buda, around where the Kings Palace used to be. This was the most exquisite very old part of Buda, with little narrow cobble-stoned streets, with gaslights and ancient houses.

We passed a house, which had a large hole on the main outside wall. The people living in it were having a meal in the front room. Through the hole we could see their feet sitting at the table. A cat, or dog, or a small child – not to mention mice and rats – could walk in and out. I couldn't believe what I had seen, and I asked Marta why had nobody repaired it?

Marta explained to me that I could not expect the hole to be repaired by the people living in the house because the house belonged to the 'State', and the State had no money to repair it.

She continued, "Anyway, why should the people living in it repair it, when it is not their own property? Why should they spend money, of which they have very little, on property which doesn't belong to them?"

So, they would rather live in a flat with a hole in it. The communist idea does kill personal incentive.

Hungarians are an industrious diligent people, but unless there is an incentive, why work harder than you have to? Everything was neglected – people's gardens, houses, streets and buildings. It was a sad first visit.

When we returned to Cardiff, I started to think about Toronto, which I found quieter, and cleaner. New York was awfully noisy and dirty. I wish I could tell you exactly how I came to the decision that I would leave Cardiff to go and live in Canada, but I just did it. My daughter was 14 years old; probably it was the worst time to move a child away from her home, friends and everything she was used to. But I did not know that at that time. I was very ambitious, and I wanted to get further than I thought I could in Cardiff, and so I applied for papers to immigrate to Canada.

By this time we had British passports, and our case was handled like the cases of average 'Brits'. I had qualifications and good references. We received our papers and started to 'liquidate' the little assets that we had. I want to mention here that I did not have to leave Lily behind, because during our time in the shop, she got married and soon after gave birth to her first child – Helen. She later had a boy – Phillip, and another boy – Andrew.

We took a ship to Canada and for the first time we were immigrants, not refugees any more. It feels different, very different. This time we actually purchased our tickets.

CHAPTER THIRTEEN

~ Another New Beginning? - Toronto & New York ~

Toronto in the 1960's was a very strange place. It was not an exciting city, it was a big provincial town with a problem – no, two problems.

Problem No. 1 was that it knew it wasn't anything as interesting as its 'sister' town Montreal, and New York, just a bit down the road, was something else again.

They called Toronto 'the city with the longest Sundays'. You couldn't do very much on Sundays; it was difficult even to get a cup of coffee. – No cinema, no nothing. In the summer, those lucky enough to be able to go 'up north' were OK. Going 'up north' meant going to one of the thousands of small lakes 'up north'. No one mentioned the name of the lake they were going to; just 'up north'.

Ontario is full of these little lakes and they are in very beautiful, mostly wooded surroundings and they are not too far away from Toronto, which makes them perfect for people to have weekend cottages on them. We were invited a few times 'up north'.

When the weather is nice these places are really great. They all have wooden patios where not only the people who are staying there congregate for meals, but also little wild animals, such as racoons, chipmunks and squirrels – they are tame, and they really enjoy the weekends when food is plentiful!

Canadians love outdoors life – summers are hot, but short and winters are great for sports, but not so wonderful in the cities.

Well, there we were in Toronto, we moved into an apartment in a brand new building on Davisville Avenue. We had received our belongings that we had taken with us (shipped separately), then purchased beds and other things needed for immediate survival. I took a tiny shop in a famous building called 'Lothian Mews'. It was an interesting building with a courtyard in the middle of it. The UNICEF statue of the little girl was standing in the centre of the courtyard.

There was also an 'Espresso-restaurant' called: "Coffee Mill" which belonged to a Hungarian lady – Marta Rubany. After opening my tiny 'boutique' and always in need of good espresso, I made friends with Marta and her husband Marci straight away. To make friends so quickly was a great help. During conversations we learned that Marci's late father was head master in the boy's high school in Kispest – where my family lived – and they always bought their soda water from my uncle.

Small world – as they say.

The little boutique was all right; I could only afford a shop upstairs so traffic was not as heavy as it would have been downstairs. I sort of managed to make a living for the two of us. Ildi enrolled in the nearest school and we both started to hate Toronto.

There were some interesting things going on in Canada at this time. People who lived in big cities, in apartments, all had to take out three-year leases. Instead of renewing a lease they all moved out and into a new building. I was surprised at this, because three years is not really long enough to make an apartment a 'home'; but then again they didn't even try. When you entered a typical Toronto apartment, you could switch on the standard lamp blindfolded and even sit down on the sofa or the two easy chairs before taking your blindfold off. They were all set in exactly the same place with an end table – coffee table height – at the end of the sofa, and basically all in the same order of furnishing.

The three yearly moves became a joke (not a very funny one). My friend, Hannah told me the following story: She and her husband were moving into a different apartment; her friend calls her and this is the conversation:

"Hannah, tell me about the new apartment?"

Hannah: "It is nice, two bedrooms, two bathrooms, balcony".
Friend: "Has the building got a pool?"

Hannah: "No pool".

Friend: "Gym, sauna, steam room?"

Hannah: "No health club".

Friend: "Doorman?"

Hannah: "No doorman".

Friend: "Why are you taking it then?"

By the year 1968 all Torontonians had to have all the above-mentioned accessories in an apartment, otherwise life was not quite complete! This did not actually apply to the poor.

I did get some publicity because I made things a little 'different', but I knew that Toronto was not for us. Had I become the 'wandering Jew'? How could I correct this mistake?

During this time a little man from India came in to sell me some Indian silks. I got friendly with him – of course – and he said that if I wanted him to, he could take me down to New York and introduce me to some people who would buy what I made. I hesitated, because of the fear of making another wrong move.

However, in 1968, "Fiddler on the Roof" was playing on Broadway with Zero Mostell in the lead. Of course I wanted to see it. I arranged with my old friends, Ella and Paul Gardos, in New York, for Ildi and me to stay with them for the Easter weekend. I had bought two tickets for the play and also for the plane. Unfortunately Martin Luther King was assassinated at this time and my friends in Toronto told me not to go because there would be violent riots in New York. We went and saw "Fiddler", and loved it.

My old friend Kathy November invited me for a lunch party on the Sunday and there were other old friends invited too. One person unknown to me was Paul. I knew his mother, his brother Peter, and Peter's family. Paul had left Hungary back in 1939, just before the war, on one of the three ocean-going cargo ships that our little country possessed. (You couldn't call the Hungarians seafarers).

His story was well known back in Kispert: Son of a Jewish dentist, after matriculating from 'gimnasium', Paul could not get into university because he was Jewish, although he had good grades. He wanted to be a doctor, as his father and older brother Peter were. However, with the help of a friend of the family – a solicitor – he got a job as a radio operator on one of those ships and left the country, officially, under the Hungarian Flag.

They went to New Orleans and Paul went up to New York on leave to visit an old friend of his father's. This wise old man talked Paul into not returning to Budapest, saying that war was imminent, and that he would always be able to get back to Hungary, but never again could he go back to the United States. This was the best advice anyone could have given a 20 year-old Hungarian Jew who would, without any doubt, have been sent to a labour camp or some other terrible place if he returned 'home'. Paul stayed, illegally.

There must have been thousands of people like Paul; young, useful to any organisation, and the American authorities quickly came to the conclusion that they could help themselves and these refugees at the same time. The solution was simple: enrol in the forces and automatically you are not only 'legalised', but also an American Citizen. This is how Paul Gaston (formerly "Gluck") became americanised overnight.

Anyway, Paul was there on Easter Sunday, 1968, at the lunch party organised in my honour and after a 20 year-old 'friendship', and after his wife died, we got married in 1988 in Bath, in England.

But, back to my little Indian silk salesman. He had talked to one of his customers in Manhattan who, when I went to see her, not only gave me a big – for me big – order for mini-dresses, skirts, etc. – all knitted on the machine, or hand crocheted – but also told me that she would help me to go down to New York to work and live.

I applied for a visa – a work permit first – and ten days later I was called into the US Consulate to receive it. A very lovely black council lady told me that she had never seen a visa cleared so fast!

Do you want to hear something really funny? On my work permit it was stated that I was a 'master tailoress'. I have never been a tailoress; in fact while I can design, cut, put things together rather well; I am absolutely incapable of sewing (to this day)!

Well, time was of great importance; I had to earn money every day of my life, so I had to move. I sold the little boutique to two Armenian sisters and Ildi came back to Cardiff. She did not want to come to New York with me, she must have been sick of my wandering. It was the first time we were separated. It was hard, very hard, and all my doing.

Sorry Ildi, I am so very sorry.

~ New York ~

I had given up the apartment. I did not even stay for the fashionable three years. Ildi came back to Britain to finish school and I was on the move once again, this time to New York.

I had temporary accommodation in a horrible small hotel on the East Side of Manhattan. Here I learned what cockroaches looked like. I started to work for Miss Suares – the woman with the boutique – in the back of the shop she had a small workroom. I knitted mini-dresses, mini-skirts, and I was very busy with special orders. She had put one of my crocheted mini-dresses in the window, and on one Saturday she took thirteen orders! The only problem was that I only had my own two hands with which to make them!

I advertised for 'homeworkers' and was totally amazed by the reaction. I had dozens of letters from women who all wanted to crochet for me. Most of all these ladies were elderly, Jewish ex-refugees from the Second World War. Back in their own 'Old Countries' they used to crochet doilies, piano and table covers, maybe even a baby's 'matinee coat' or two.

Some of them started to work with me and stayed until they were too old to continue. They were from Vienna, Berlin, Budapest, Prague, etc., very cultured, civilised old ladies, happy not only to make a little money, but also mostly to feel useful again. There was a Hungarian lady: Gisella Stern, who not only reminded me of my own 'Auntie Gisi', but her husband's name, was Joseph, too!

We made friends immediately and she started to bring me presents. I kept on saying that she spent more on me than I paid her, but even at her last visit, she presented me with something nice. She became very ill and passed away. I missed her for years.

I left the horrible hotel with its cockroaches and I moved into a furnished apartment on the corner of Third Avenue and Fiftieth Street. I worked for Ilka, Miss Suares, for about 6-7 months, when Paul and I realised that it was silly for me not to make the money for myself that I was making for 'my boss'. I started my own designing and manufacturing business in 1970.

My first two customers were two British guys, who had a very nice boutique in the back of the – then – Vidal Sassoon beauty salon on famous Madison Avenue. They bought quite nicely and took special orders.

I received publicity in the 'Bible of the Rag Trade' – the name of this daily paper is 'Women's Wear Daily', a Fairchild publication. The – then – editor liked what I made and 'wrote me up' a few times. Shops started to order and I was in business (again)!

Besides privately owned boutiques, I started to get into some great department stores, like Bergdorf Goodman, Bonvit & Teller and later Saks Fifth Avenue. I also started to sell to Jordan Marsh in Florida, Joseph Magnin in San Francisco, the Bullocks stores in Los Angeles and 5 or 6 other towns in Southern California, etc. Later I got in to the high-class salons of Elizabeth Arden, in New York and Miami.

One of the big sensations for me during my first years in business was travel to the most important cities in the country to do shows in stores, known in the trade as 'Trunk Shows'.

The name comes from the time when travelling salesmen were going around the States; they took their 'Trunks' with them. In the shop – or store – they opened their trunks, took out all their goods, and the owner or manager would invite their good customers for a glass of wine, and some stock would be sold and orders taken.

The idea behind these shows was that as no shop could buy a whole collection, the salesman and/or designer – comes along, shows everything they have and it is pure profit for the shop and for the manufacturer.

I was invited to Jordan Marsh, Miami Beach, to do my first 'Trunk show' and it was just wonderful. I took lots of orders and even developed one or two good customers. To be perfectly honest, I loved every moment of it.

After the first Trunk show, I did many others. I was lucky to be able to travel quite a lot. I saw many interesting places, some beautiful, some exciting, and some awfully boring. The little business was getting a bit bigger and by 1972 I was doing well. Some of my private customers were great, and every one recommended me to someone new. One of these ladies was a tiny pint sized woman and her name was Lee Leon. Her husband – Sol Leon – was, and still is, one of the senior partners of the famous William Morris Agency in Los Angeles.

They were the largest, and I think most important agency dealing with the big stars in Hollywood. Lee was a very good customer and a very nice person. We made her not only day, but evening outfits as well, and I was very proud because she wore some of them to the 'Oscars' ceremonies over several years.

She first brought in her identical twin sister, called Joyce, whose daughter Andrea was about to marry Mark Gershwin, the only son of the three Gershwin brothers. I was asked to make the wedding outfits for all the ladies in the wedding party.

Back in 1952, when I received the 78rpm record of George Gershwin's 'Rhapsody in Blue', I wouldn't have even dreamed about actually working for a member of that very famous family.

I was just thinking about the slogan "you came a long way, baby..." I did, didn't I?

Well, the same Lee Leon brought the lovely Dionne Warwick to see me. She was already a mega star, but you could not tell that from her behaviour: she was friendly, nice with no pretence and no showing off – just a very nice woman.

Dionne came into the workroom and let me introduce her to all the girls. We then had lunch with all of them at the long table – off paper plates. After that she went to the shelves on which we had hundreds of cones of yarn, in all conceivable colours, and said: "Mady, you know the suit I like; make me one in each of these colours". With that she handed me nine cones! She wanted nine suits made!

She had, and still has a stunning body; so working with her was a real pleasure for me. She invited me to several of her concerts in and around New York; it was very 'different' to walk in as guests of the star.

In about 1974 I had a new customer who turned out to be Stephen Sondheim's mother. She became a good customer and I used to listen to her stories, all either about her very talented son who at that time was becoming famous, but also about the 'Rag Trade' in the old days. Her former husband, the father of Stephen was a coat manufacturer and she had some very funny stories to tell. People in the 'Rag Trade' were like the real New York taxi drivers, full of funny stories.

One day she came in to see me and asked for a favour. She told me that she had this very old friend whose husband was in hospital, about to have an operation to remove a brain tumour. She also told me that this friend was facing some very serious financial problems due to the terrible price of being sick in the United States, and could I possibly buy some jewellery from the little boutique she was running in her apartment. I, of course, agreed to go and see this lady. My appointment was on a beautiful Saturday afternoon. It was in December, a very cold but sunny day. I bought a red rose for her, as I did not know what she liked since I didn't even know who she was.

The apartment was on the very fashionable Central Park South. I was 'announced' by the doorman, and let in by a beautiful young woman, who said: "You must be Mady; I will tell my aunt that you are here".

The door of the living room opened, and a tiny blonde lady, absolutely beautiful, although not young, greeted me and ushered me into a lovely elegant room, where Mrs Leshin, Stephen Sondheim's mother was sitting. My lovely hostess asked me what I would like to drink. I asked for a cup of coffee.

She said that coffee was not good for me, but would I like a glass of champagne instead?

I said, "Please do not open a bottle for me", to which she replied, "Darling, there is always a bottle open in the icebox – actually there are two bottles, so that when one is finished there is an immediate replacement"!

After she went to the kitchen, Mrs. Leshin told me that the beautiful lady's husband had died early that morning. I asked her why she had not called me to stop me from coming. Our hostess came back at that moment and said that she needed friends there to help her get through the day. This was her second husband, the big love of her life, and she was completely distraught.

While we were having our champagne, which she told us was very important for the complexion of "us girls" I started to notice several pictures of a beautiful young woman on the walls. I still did not know who my hostess was. Then in the course of the conversation it came out that her husband, who had just died, was a former head of one of the big film studios in Hollywood.

Well, it came out that this remarkable little lady was, in fact, Carmel Myers, a former silent movie star, who had been the star of the first Ben Hur film, back in 1927.

She told us the story of her father, who was a Jewish Rabbi in Beverly Hills (the first one, I think). The studio, planning to make the film went to him to ask if he would give them instructions so that the religious side of the film would be correct. The rabbi was very willing and gave them the direction they needed. When they asked him for his bill, he told them that he didn't want money, but that what he wanted was a screen test for Carmel, who was about 17 or 18 years old at that time. She was determined to become a movie star and he was convinced that this would get it out of her system. To his biggest shock, she got the part!

She must have been absolutely beautiful as the young star of the film; because at the time I met her she was still gorgeous. She still had a wonderful complexion, with no make up, her eyes were beautiful and she was just stunning in her eighties!

I not only bought a big bunch of her jewellery to help her, but also met her several times after this very memorable first meeting. A few years after this Carmel returned to Los Angeles, and I did not see her after that.

CHAPTER FOURTEEN

~ Life in New York ~

I have just realised that I have not mentioned the place I was living in by this time. I had an apartment on the corner of '89th and Madison' meaning the corner of 89th street and Madison Avenue. My place was on the 14th floor, which in this country would be 13th floor, but because Americans are – at least many of them – superstitious – after the 12th floor, the 14th floor follows.

So, I was living in this 41-story apartment building, in a two-bedroom apartment. It was almost new when I moved in, and it was great with the most super details: Two bathrooms and enough 'closets' – walk-in ones and just regular ones – to house ten times as much 'stuff' than I had, although by this time I had accumulated a lot. Being in the fashion business it is easy to get something whenever one feels that one 'needs' something new, because it really would be bad to wear something old to a function. After all, one has to advertise ones new styles.

But back to the apartment. On the 41st floor we had a swimming pool with a glass roof, which they opened in the summer, a sunroof, and also a sauna. Such luxury!

The building is one block away from Central Park and from my tiny balcony I looked on to the roof of the famous Guggenheim Museum. I lived a short six blocks away from the Metropolitan Museum of Art. I loved walking to the Museum on Saturday mornings, when New Yorkers go to all the many museums. To watch people on weekends, dressed in totally different clothes from the 'during the week, going to business' outfits was really something special – jeans, sweatshirts and always sneakers.

The beautiful 'Frick Museum' is on the corner of Fifth Avenue and 70th Street and that was also a favourite place for me to walk to on a nice Saturday morning. My everlasting love for museums was well satisfied while living in New York, not to mention the special occasions when I had a few days in Washington DC, the home of the world famous Smithsonian Institute.

During my life in New York the Hungarians held some 'cultural' evenings. Some of these occasions were more cultural than others. One of the better ones was on a Sunday afternoon. There were two entertainers – a George Mikes from London and a George Feyer from New York.

Let me tell you about George Mikes first. Mr. Mikes was a Hungarian Jew who was sent to London to cover the Munich crisis as a correspondent. He had a doctorate in Law, but he became a journalist. He came to Britain for a fortnight, but stayed forever! During the war he was engaged to broadcast to Hungary and during the Hungarian Revolution he was sent back to cover it for the BBC.

After the war he became a critic and a writer. He wrote a great number of books, but the most popular ones were his stories he wrote of the many countries he had visited. These were not 'traveller's' stories, but stories about the people of those countries, and he was always taking the 'mickey' out of them. For instance:

'How to be an Alien' – about the foreigners living in Britain. The funniest line in that book is where he describes the difference between the Brits and those living on the 'Continent', He said something like: "Continental people have sex lives and the British people take hot water bottles to bed"!

He also wrote 'How to Scrape Skies' about New York; 'How to Unite Nations'; 'How to Tango' about South America, and many more.

So, there we were at the Hungarian Sunday afternoon cultural event, with the two George's entertaining us, and it was a super afternoon! The other George, George Feyer was a superb pianist and entertainer, and also, by this time, a good friend.

George Feyer, his lovely wife Jolie, Paul and I bought the – until then – most expensive theatre tickets to see the Royal Shakespeare Company performing Dickens's Nicholas Nickleby. The tickets cost $100 each! You could choose between going two evenings or you could see it in its full length on a Saturday. We opted for the latter. I think we had something like three and half-hours before lunch and about the same afterwards. The restaurant opposite the little theatre had never done so much business before or since!

The play was one of the most memorable of all the many plays I had the pleasure of seeing. The story, of course, I think is one of Dickens's best. The cast were wonderful, actors coming into the auditorium, mingling with the people, something we had never experienced before. By the time we came out we all said that it was worth every penny of the $100!

One day, also in the early seventies, I returned to the workshop at about 10-11am, from an early morning Fashion show. Upon entering the little office, I looked at Celeste and Susie, the then Supervisor, and asked: "what is wrong? You both look as if someone has been murdered"

They insisted on me sitting down and having a cup of tea. They then told me that my very old friend from Budapest, Ella Gardos had telephoned, to tell me that her husband Paul had been stabbed on their way home very early that morning, and had later died in hospital.

I immediately went to her apartment, which was on 104th on the west side of Manhattan. It was very close to the Columbia University, and was already a dangerous neighbourhood. Soon after I had arrived the Police also arrived, and because of the terrible state my old friend was in I had the very awful job of telling them what had happened.

The story was that the two of them, both in their sixties, were returning from the little Hungarian Restaurant they owned in the 'Hungarian District' of Manhattan, namely 2nd Avenue, in the 80's. They used one of those lock-up garages, just a few blocks away from the street where they lived. After getting out to the street having parked and closed the garage, some men jumped Paul, stabbed him several times after he had already given them all his money, several thousand dollars. They pushed Ella down to the ground where she passed out. This saved her life as they thought she was dead, so they ran away. Ella managed to hail a taxi, and got Paul to the nearby hospital, where he passed away a few hours later. The detective in charge told me that they must have been Colombians. When I asked how he knew, he said that the killers from the Colombian Republic always take the loot first and kill afterwards.

Let me tell you about this tragic little, kind, and warm-hearted man. My old friend Paul Gardos was a talented textile engineer. He went through the old fashioned way of getting a trade. He first became a weaver, and because he wanted to better his life, he then went to college and got his degree. Ella and Paul had no children, but he always had a job, textiles being an important trade in Hungary, and the two of them lived reasonably well. However, Paul never wanted to leave the Old Country, but Ella did. She managed to talk Paul into leaving and they, like so many others, mostly Jewish Hungarians, settled in New York. I think, like so many others the two of them were totally disillusioned after a few hard years. As I said earlier, New York streets are not paved with gold, and making a living in a strange, very hard city was not easy. Paul tried to get a job, but even with his excellent qualifications and knowledge of the language, he had no luck. They decided to open the awful little restaurant where poor Ella was the cook. In time it became a sort of meeting place of the Hungarians. They even imported entertainers from 'back home', but the place was really sad. When I arrived in New York, years after they had opened the place I felt really very sorry for these hardworking decent people to have had to do a job like that. I found it demeaning and I was sure they did too, but there was no other way out. They must have been in debt and we feared that since the rumour was that all small restaurants were involved with the Mafia, they were too. When Paul was murdered, we all wondered if it was the Mafia that had him killed. The police actually caught two of the men and poor Ella had to identify them, which she did. The fact that Paul had survived one of the concentration camps, then against his will went to the 'Land of Opportunities', only to get stabbed to death, seemed (and it still does) totally unfair to me. Much later somehow, Ella got over this terrible tragedy, but never got over his death, and we all knew that she was still paying for the years she spent in the miserable little kitchen in her restaurant called 'Monkey Bar'. She died many years later in Florida, still working in the kitchen of a restaurant. She was then close to 80 years old. America did not give her an easy life either.

One of the wealthier Hungarians, 1938 refugees, was a couple called Nanasi. Mrs. Nanasi, Jolan, phoned me once and told me that she was sending me two potential customers. One for them was Jolie Gabor, 'the Mother of all Gabors' and the other was a woman whose only claim to fame was that she was also Hungarian.

Let me deal with the 'other' woman first. She came into the showroom, asked for me and told me that she wants to order some suits. She was demanding and quite arrogant, so Celeste and I took an instant dislike to her. I told her that we could take her orders and quoted some prices. She stated that she expected to pay wholesale prices! I told her that it would be all right to do that if she had a shop. Of course she didn't have a shop, but she demanded to get the discount because she came from the same country as I!

I replied, "Madame, everybody knows that the supermarket chain's boss, Mr. D'Agustino is Italian. Do you think that all Italians get their groceries wholesale?"

She did not like me either, and it was proof that we Hungarians don't automatically love each other!

Now, I will get to the 'important one' Madame Gabor, recommended by Mrs. Nanasi, which was very odd by itself, because Mrs. Nanasi never ordered or bought anything from me herself, although I was no more expensive than any other designer. Her husband was a clever man who was a special lighting manager in the theatre world and made lots of money. The reason that she recommended me was as I mentioned before, that while Italians, Chinese, Polish and all other people will support each other, Hungarians will only go to another 'Hunkie' if it is good for them.

Anyway, Madame Gabor arrived at maybe 11am, on the arm of a 28-year-old, 8ft tall all-American bodyguard – (they are all 28 years old and 8 feet tall!). It was a very cold winter's day and Jolie was dressed in a white mink coat, the type that has black tips on the ends of the fur. This is not flattering for someone who is very short and not very slim. To add insult to injury the coat was double-breasted! As if this was not enough, she also wore a hat made out of the same mink, with a very wide brim, which is also not recommended for short ladies. With all due respect to her she did look like a huge mushroom!

Now, I have to say that I was worried about her visit because I knew that she would not buy anything and that it would not be easy for me to deal with her. You see Jolie had a reputation for not paying her bills. She felt, like so many other celebrities do, that they are above paying for their goods – why should they? Only ordinary people pay! (Like Mrs. Hemsley said: "Only poor people pay taxes"!)

Well, Jolie Gabor was in my showroom and I was not excited about it. She took off the white mink coat and, to my horror, she had on a pair of knitted, tight ribbed trousers, in black Lurex, with a matching 'poor boy' sweater, fashionable in those days for the young and slim. Sadly, as she was in her eighties, she was neither.

After trying on some clothes she said to me that she thought $200 was a lot of money to pay for a dress, to which my answer was that the dress was not $200, but $400!

That was the moment when she started to explain to me what a privilege it would be for me, who is so new in the business, to make clothes for the Gabors. I told her that I knew it would be a great honour, but that I could not afford it yet!

This was the moment when I knew that it was not only me who did not like her, but that the feeling was mutual. At this point, the bodyguard who had been sitting in the 'Caddy' (Cadillac) came up to say that he had to move 'it', because he was being chased away by the police. Madame Gabor started to get ready to leave but could not resist telling me about the book she was in the middle of writing. I made the mistake of telling her that I knew about the book, because I knew her 'ghost' writer.

She started to tell me about a little bit in the book. It went like this:

Jolie was in the park, aged four, with her 'Fraulein' (Austrian Au Pair), and her cousin Jonny was also in the park with his Fraulein. Jonny had an apple and Jolie asked if he would give her a bite out of it. Jonny, also aged four said that he would let her have a bite of his apple if she would pull down her knickers and show him what she had there.

I, compounding my mistake, asked: "And did you show him, Madame Gabor?"

She did not answer. However before she departed she told me that (in case I didn't know) she was older than I was, and reminded me that she had three grown up daughters. I told her that I also had a grown up daughter, but did not point out to her that her youngest daughter was 10 - 13 years older than I was!

This was the beginning and end of my could-have-been relationship with the famous Gabors.

A new customer was recommended to me whose name was Lynne Meisler. She was employed by an organisation called 'Brotherhood of Christians and Jews'. It was a great idea and the meetings were very interesting. What it tried to do was to get together all religions and to celebrate great humanitarians who deserved to get an award for the wonderful things they did for humanity.

Lynne was one of the people who actually worked with the celebrities and liased with the PR people. She also organised the gala dinners themselves.

The dinners were always held in one of the great hotels in New York, and after Lynne came to me first to have her outfits made for these very special occasions, she always gave me two tickets for each of these truly wonderful events. She never ordered anything from other designers after she started to buy my clothes.

The last dinner I had the privilege of attending was for the New York politician, Jacob Javits, who by this time was tragically sitting in a wheelchair, managing only to speak through one of those terrible boxes, used by victims of a debilitating illness where they lose their vocal cords.

After a few years of attending these dinners it all tragically stopped. My lovely friend, Lynne, was already suffering with terminal stomach cancer, which I was not to know. Her husband, Michael told me she was on chemotherapy. She had always told me that she had an ulcer. Lynne died only a week after she came to me for dinner. I knew she had just had a treatment and was feeling terrible, but she did not complain, and would not admit to dying.

Just a few months after her funeral, I asked Michael when he would be going back to work – he was selling perfumes, the finest imports. He told me that since Lynne had died he had become lazy and did not care anymore. To my great shock he died from the cancer from which he had been suffering long before Lynne had discovered that she was so drastically, terminally ill. Their two daughters lost both parents within three or four months.

The originator of this organisation, many years before was actually an Englishman, whose name I cannot remember, unfortunately. He must have been a great and optimistic man to try to do something about getting people to see how wonderful the world could be if they would sit together in one room and celebrate together, regardless of religion or race.

The organisation was absolutely non-profit making, but the invited all had to pay a lot of money for the tickets. I think to 'buy a plate' must have been several hundred dollars.

I remember one of the recipients of the Award was the great Walter Cronkyde, who by this time was a legend in the field of communications. There was another marvellous man, Danny Kaye, who was also great and very entertaining.

The totally unusual thing about these dinners was that several priests from different religions were seated at the Dias together. One would perhaps do the blessing, maybe another one would speak, but everything was done as if all of these 'men of the church' were of the same persuasion.

We all thought, or at least I did, that if this feeling of brotherhood could be made more popular – that if people could go to each other's churches, synagogues or temples to pray, or even just to get to know each other, then this world would be a much nicer place to live in.

CHAPTER FIFTEEN

~ Business is Good ~

One of my trips took me to Atlanta, Georgia, a great city with stunning ladies, real 'Southern belles', coming to see me at the 'Saks Fifth Avenue' store. I was in the 'designers room', which gave me some clout.

A beautiful young girl – 20ish – arrived with her equally beautiful mother – around 40 – 42 years; and the mother's mother, a gorgeous 62-year-old woman. This was graduation week; the town was all decorated and looked very festive. The young girl bought a knitted evening dress from me, the mother too and then the grandmother also. All of these were to be worn at the biggest Graduation Ball in Atlanta.

This would have been wonderful enough, but they even took an outfit for the great-grandmother, aged 84 years! I must admit it was a good feeling to be able to satisfy four generations of great looking women from the same family.

This was especially good, because in the fashion trade the age of the customer makes a big difference, so we proved that our clothes were 'ageless'.

It must have been about this time when I received a Design Award from the 'Retail Fashion Authorities of America for Creative Achievement in the Women's Knitwear Industry'. The award was very prestigious. Unfortunately it does not bring in the kind of money that an 'Oscar' does, but I did feel very proud about getting it. However, after all these years it only looks good when it is printed on my Curriculum Vitae.

I must mention here that soon after I started the little business I became a member of the 'Couture Group'. This was, as its name suggests, a group of designers in the higher category of the fashion market. One of its advantages was that twice a year they organised for the group to hold their shows in the same place on the same days. The first of these shows I ever participated in was held in the famous Waldorf Astoria Hotel on Park Avenue. My PR (public relations) girl, Bobby, came to me a few minutes before we were due to start and asked if I was ready.

I replied: "The models are ready, made up, hair done and dressed; the music is coming through; various people are running around with ear phones and walkie-talkies; I don't have to be ready, everything else is!"

She said: "Don't be silly, Mady, you are the compere of your show!"

I answered her: "If you send me out there, I'll die"

She replied: "Just go out there, look around the audience and think that all their bodily functions are the same as yours, then start to talk!"

I did just that, and I must tell you that this was one of the most useful pieces of advice anyone has ever given me! (Incidentally, I have used this method lots of times since, and now when I talk to groups of ladies as an 'After Lunch speaker' I find it very easy.)

After this first Fashion Show, a lovely lady from the 'New York Post' newspaper, (the biggest afternoon paper), called and came to look at my collection. Her name was Ruth Preston, and she was Beauty and Fashion Editor for about thirty years. She liked what she saw and she also liked me. She was the only fashion writer who, if she could not say something nice, would rather not write about you at all.

Ruth was very good to me and I had write-ups often. This, of course, goes further than one article in the Post, because other papers pick it up, so I had interviews with all kinds of papers from various parts of the country. When you did a show in, say, Chicago, if you were lucky a fashion editor would come to the store you were in for an interview and if she was syndicated you got lots of publicity.

Ruth Preston and I were lunching in the famous 'Russian Tea-room', next door to Carnegy Hall, and she told me that she wanted me to meet a good friend of hers, who was a very stylish PR lady. At the time of the appointment I welcomed a stunning woman of about 55 – 58 years, quite exotic looking, with gorgeous green almond shaped eyes, dressed in white linen trousers, a fabulous navy linen jacket and a white turban with 3 or 4 gold turtles pinned on to the turban. She was well made up and looked very different from most of the women working in the business as writers or PR. They usually wore old depressing clothes, bad hair, without make up, and certainly not representing 'high fashion'.

This stunning lady: Vera Bacall – married name Mrs. Ira Koenig – was born in Russia, went to the States just before the war (lucky lady), spoke excellent English with a very slight accent, and we were friends by the end of the appointment. She took me on as a client.

Vera also represented – amongst others – the well-known Gottex Swimwear Company from Israel. 'Gottex' was the brand name, the owner and designer was a Mrs. Gottlieb from Budapest, and they made – and still do – very expensive, very stylish beach and swimwear. Vera was also PR for her best friend Madam Potok, the owner and designer of the also world famous Maximillian Fur Company.

Let me tell you about Madam Potok: Anna (Anoushka to her friends), and I became 'best friends' the minute she came into my showroom the first time. She was tiny, blonde, with a gorgeous complexion, which never saw a drop of make-up, and even at her age – 70ish – looked superb. She stepped in and I said, "Madame Potok, I already love you!"

She did look a bit puzzled, and so I said: "You are shorter than I am, so I have to love you!"

A wonderful friendship developed with a truly fantastic lady. She and her brother Maximillian fled from Warsaw in the early '30's, and went to Paris where they continued their trade making fabulous fur coats for the 'elite' women of the world. They left Paris, went to New York, opened a salon in 57th Street, just off Fifth Avenue, and made coats for 'everybody who was anybody'. I went to visit her in her salon many times, not only to see her, but also to witness fittings she made on the house models. This was on coats for people such as: Sophia Loren, Audrey Hepburn, The Shah of Iran's wife, Farah Diba; all the important stars and celebrities, and also, I think many royal ladies.

Sophia Loren and her husband Carlo Ponti were staying in one of the top hotels, and I was dying from envy, when a phone call came to ask Anoushka to send some coats up to the hotel for Miss Loren to try on. Because she knew it was going to be a surprise from Miss Loren's husband, Anoushka decided to go to the hotel herself. She told me that to fit Miss Loren with a coat has always given her great pleasure. She also said that Sophia was one of the most beautiful women in the world, with the greatest figure.

Anoushka was incredible. She would notice a 1/8th-inch difference between two shoulders on a fox fur coat. She was a true artist and actually had a son who was an artist. He was a good painter and all would have been great, but the son, Andrew inherited a condition that makes victims of it blind. Another great lady who never hurt anyone, with another tragedy. Why?

But back to my famous customers.

I received an invitation from a private customer, a very 'posh' interior decorator who was in partnership with Mrs Victor Borge's daughter. The invitation was for a cocktail party being held in their offices in one of the most famous new buildings, called 'Atrium' on the wonderful 57th Street East. The woman knew that I was crazy about Victor Borge and said that I could meet Mrs. Borge if I came. I sure went!

Mrs. Borge (Sannah) was a tall, beautiful woman. After I had been introduced, I said to her: "Mrs Borge, I want you to know that I have been in love with your husband for 20 years!"

She said: "Oh, how wonderful darling, so have I!"

She became a customer and a few months after I had met her I told her that I would love to meet Mr. Borge. The next time she came for a fitting, the 'elevator' door opened and there was Mr. Borge, standing next to Sannah. She turned to her husband and said: "Victor, darling, this is Mady who has been in love with you for over 20 years!"

He turned to me and said "I didn't know this, why doesn't someone tell me these things…?"

Mr. Borge, sadly no longer with us, was not only a super entertainer and a truly funny man, but also a very attractive man. I started to go to his shows every time he came to Manhattan and whenever he had a show around New York. His 'One Man Show' was always a sell-out. One time I had two tickets – for Paul and myself – and by the time Vera Bacall tried to book the tickets were all gone. It was a Saturday evening, and on the Sunday Vera called me on the telephone and asked me about the show. I started to 'recite' and after about an hour and a half, Vera said to her husband who had listened on the extension; "It is not such a tragedy, darling that we did not get tickets; sitting at home comfortably we have now heard the whole show!"

I told this story to Mrs Borge the next time I saw her and she said: "How wonderful, Mady! I will tell Victor that the next time he has laryngitis you can stand behind him and be his voice!"

On another one of these occasions, Mr. Borge again came in with Sannah who was having a fitting for some clothes we were making for her. During our coffee together he told me that he had just returned from Britain where he had one of his concerts in Cardiff, remembering that I had lived in that city, and in fact that was where I saw him first in the early '60's. This is what he said.

"Mady dear, Cardiff has changed hugely, you will see this when you go back next time".

I said: "Tell me, what is the great change?"

Mr. Borge: "You know that I always stay in the Angel Hotel? Guess what, they had an actual light fitting, hanging from the ceiling in my room!"

Me: "What did they have before?"

Mr. Borge: "A bulb, hanging on the end of a wire…!"

I heard some wonderful stories about this incomparable man, who achieved the highest success, not only as an entertainer, but also as a human being. We made Mr. Borge a knitted – machine, but quite thick – black chenille double breasted smoking jacket. When he received it he sent me a card, saying, "I can hardly wait for the cold weather to put it on!"

The last time I met him, I took my two grandchildren to New York, where I spoke to James Colias, Mr. Borge's secretary and 'Man Friday'. There was a concert in Connecticut and they sent me four tickets. He was in his late 80's and as good as ever. My grandchildren really enjoyed meeting him. He loved children and had many grandchildren himself.

I still miss him, although I did not see him often. After his beautiful Sannah died, he lost the will to live and wanted to join her. He achieved that too, just about three months after she died. His dedicated photo is in the hall of my cottage and I look at him every day.

One of my great customers had been running a boutique in her house in Washington DC. The boutique was in the very luxurious basement of their house. I went to do shows for her a few times and once I asked if a shop was allowed in the very select, very residential neighbourhood they lived in.

She said: "Don't worry, my dear. Mr. Hoover lives on the corner, and he is friendly with my husband and often comes for dinner". Mr. Hoover, of course was the head of the FBI. (Important neighbour to have!)

I was also very honoured to be invited a few times to St. Angelo, Texas, where the American Mohair Growers had their headquarters. I was the guest speaker and they gave me a fantastic time. However, before I got to the tiny St. Angelo in a small commuter plane – scary – I arrived in Houston's super airport. It reminded me of the time before, when I went to Houston to do a show and had to take a taxi. I got into it and the driver was one of those gorgeous-looking elderly Southern black men, friendly and helpful. He asked me, as we were driving up to the store I had to go to, how I liked Houston. I said that I had never seen such a huge sky in my life before! It was blue, sparkling, and very impressive. The nice old driver immediately handed me his call card and told me that a nice lady like me should not live in a 'hellish place' like New York. He said that I should move to Houston and that I could live with him and his wife for a period until I got myself an apartment! I did thank him, but did not take up his offer!

Well, during my 'speech' at the Mohair Growers' dinner party – in my honour, may I add – I mentioned this, and when I received the 'thank you' letter from them, they promised that the next time I went down, they would show me "even more sky"!

Everything was smashing; the only problem I had was that all the Texans appeared to be 8 - 9 feet tall, and I was very short even then! (I am even shorter now). I really enjoyed Texas – the people were very substantial, very understated and low key. When I asked some of them how many Mohair goats they had (mohair comes off the coats of goats, not sheep), they very modestly said "50 – 60 thousand, or was it 500 – 600 thousand?" (Not a great difference!)

This reminds me of the old story: Bar in Texas; young, tall Californian stands at the bar with a drink in his hand and tells everyone around him that he has a ranch called 'Setting Sun', thousands of acres, millions of cattle, goats, sheep, etc. No one is listening. He keeps throwing his weight about, no one cares. He notices a smallish Texan, middle-aged, dressed in an impeccable suit with wonderful alligator skin cowboy boots, etc., but all in good taste. The young 'show-off' turns to the Texan and says: "Tell me, don't you have any real estate?"

The man says, very quietly, "Yes, I do have some real estate".

The young man says, "Well, tell me what your ranch is called, and how many acres you have?"

The Texan answers: "12 acres, and it is called Down Town Houston!"

Back in New York, my two – by this time – best friends and I went to one of the Fashion shows held early in the morning. This particular one was in the Hilton Hotel. It was just a few weeks after Ruth Preston lost her husband after 5 – 6 years in a wheelchair as a result of a massive stroke. He was a medical doctor.

Anyway, Ruth was telling us that Esther Hamburger – a legend in the fashion business – a fashion writer – called her to say how sorry she was about Bob's passing. She – Esther – then said to Ruth: "Ruth dear, now that you will be living by yourself, you will have to be very careful to talk to yourself in full sentences. Don't worry, we all talk to ourselves, but you have to give yourself the same courtesy you are giving to friends – full sentences, please. Don't say to yourself 'OK, Ruth'. Explain whatever you are talking about…"

We killed ourselves laughing it was so funny! As we went out after the show, the first person we met was Miss Hamburger. I said to her: "Ruth has just told us what you said about talking to herself".

She turned to me, and said: "Mady dear, you live alone too. You also have to be careful, talk properly – to yourself – we, you and I (she was a German Jewess) owe it to this wonderful language we have adopted, to speak properly, even to ourselves".

There was someone else I had also made friends with after I started the business, another Hungarian woman – her name: Judith Leiber. Judy is one of the most talented people I have ever met. She – now retired – has designed and manufactured the world's most exclusive handbags and belts ever. Her bags are carried by all the glamorous stars and celebrities in the world. Most famous are her jewelled evening bags. I am lucky to have several of her gorgeous ostrich leather bags, all unbelievably beautiful.

Judy met Gus Leiber, an American GI, in Budapest after the war. They married; Judy followed her husband to New York, and started to design and manufacture her exclusive handbags and belts, and her name became the name of a legend.

Judy has worked very hard for many years and has built a fantastic business. Her husband, Gus is a well-known painter, very modern, from the Picasso-style school. They have a wonderful marriage; they complement each other in taste for the arts, for the visual and also for the performing arts.

She had a miniature United Nations in her workshops and her enviable talent to speak seven or eight languages made it easier for her to deal with all her employees. We had a bartering system. I made her knitted, crocheted garments and she paid me with bags! They are all beautiful. Many of Judy's handbags are already collectors' items. I feel proud to know them both.

During the first few months in New York I went – with some newly made friends – to the Metropolitan Museum of Art. As we walked through the fantastic large and wonderful main lobby, we went to the coffee shop. I of course, wanted coffee – and there in the centre of this huge 'room' was a sunken area with dozens of modern statues, all made into working fountains. I immediately recognised Karl Milles's work and said this to my friends. They looked at me as if to say, "You are bluffing, aren't you?" So I made them go closer to the display and sure enough, Karl Milles's name was on it. It was several years before that I saw Milles's garden exhibition in Stockholm and was pleased to see these wonderful pieces of art again.

My little business started to 'get off the ground'. About two years or so after I had started my business, I had a phone call to tell me that Claire Booth Luce wanted to come and see me. Mrs. Luce was an elderly lady, tall, very handsome and very elegant.

Claire Booth Luce was the widow of the famous publisher, Mr. Luce, and a very outstanding woman in her own right. She was the only female ambassador of the USA in Europe during the Second World War. She was sent to Italy and served there. By the time I met her she was living in Hawaii and came up to New York to visit her stepson and his family. She ordered several outfits; some of them for evening wear. I used to love to sit in the fantastic duplex apartment of her stepson, and for hours would listen to her stories.

CHAPTER SIXTEEN

~ Eccentricities of New York ~

Life in New York was really wonderful because I tried to do a great number of things that I really enjoyed doing, not only going to the theatre, and to the Opera, but I even purchased a season ticket for the Philharmonic. I went with my (by this time) much loved Vera and her husband Ira every time our ticket 'came up' and we certainly heard some wonderful music. The main conductor, in fact the Musical Director, was the gorgeous looking Zubin Mehta. I remember talking with Vera and other female friends about him and we had to admit that watching Mr. Mehta was almost more important to us than the music that the great orchestra provided. Mr. Mehta made all of us look forward to the next concert very much, to see him and to hear the music, I must admit in that order!

One year we had a concert to go to in the beginning of May. I knew that the beautiful dark mink cape Ira had ordered for Vera for the previous Christmas from Maximillian Furs had just been delivered a few days before the first of May. The reason for the long delay was the fact that Madam Potok, our beloved Anoushka, was a real perfectionist, which meant that every little piece of a coat had to be perfectly matched. We were all in awe of the craftsmanship of this tiny lady and while we were sure that nobody, with the exception of Madam Potok could notice any 'imperfection' as she used to call them, she could not have a coat delivered unless she said it was perfect.

So, back to Ira's fabulously beautiful Christmas present; it was delivered four months late because it took a little longer than usual for the furs to be perfectly matched. I spoke to Vera before getting ready for the concert, only to find out what she was going to wear, and I was surprised to hear on the phone that she said: "Darling, my new mink, naturally".

I said, "but darling, it is 84 degrees in the shade, will you not be too hot?"

To which my totally eccentric friend replied "But darling, I have to wear it once, before it goes into storage!"

Of course all real furs had to go into cold storage for the summer. (We don't have these kinds of problems now, because we don't wear fur any more.)

Vera, in all aspects, was a real female. Not only was she always ‘put together’ exceptionally well, but she made sure that her make up, her accessories, her gold turtles decorating the ‘trade mark’ turban, everything, always created her ‘total look’ perfectly.

Often we were complaining that it was too cold out and we were going out in some flimsy clothing, or it was too hot and we felt that we had on the wrong outfit to feel comfortable. Vera always said, “Darling, one has to be willing to suffer in order to look gorgeous!” And we did.

I did a number of shows in various places, which was a great way for me to see many places in the States, places where I would not have a chance to visit otherwise. Chicago, the “Windy City”, became my favourite, not only because it was good for my little business and I developed some very nice accounts, but because of the special beauty of that city. Lake Michigan comes into the bottom of Michigan Avenue and in the summer it is unbelievably picturesque, looking onto the colourful boats. It really takes your breath away.

I was taken out to dinner one evening and my hosts took me to the Hotel Drake, where in the very famous Restaurant I tasted my first potato skin with delicious melted cheese. (I cooked it for a dinner party back in the apartment later on and my Hungarian friend, Ella Gardos, told me that I was wasting all the good potato!)

Now that I have told you how wonderful Chicago is in the summer, let me tell you that in the winter this becomes a totally different story.

I had to go to Chicago in the month of February to do a 'Trunk Show'. I remember arriving on a bleak Sunday evening, soon after the city suffered a massive snowstorm. I needed a taxi to take me to my hotel, but to my biggest surprise, there were none. I waited for exactly 27 minutes and I was getting very seriously cold. I had on a long fur coat, fur hat, fur scarf, and warm boots! The famous Chicago winds were blowing a gale, and I remember thinking how crazy life is. I had survived concentration camps, and I’d got as far as the Chicago airport. I was wearing mink from top to bottom and I was going to freeze to death on a Sunday evening on my way to a luxury hotel! (The shop, which had invited me, always put me into super hotels).

As if by magic taxis started to arrive and eventually I was lifted into the back of a cab by a very friendly elderly black southern driver. He measured up my frozen condition and immediately offered me a cup of hot tea! After a few minutes I actually managed to talk again and asked him why there had been no taxis for such a long time.

He explained that as there was a snowstorm and those Sunday evenings were usually quiet, they all went home! Then I asked what the temperature was, to which he replied: "Honey, you don't want to know!"

I said that I really would like him to tell me, and so he did. It was 35 degrees below freezing point! Luckily it included the wind-chill factor!

I did get to the gorgeous hotel where I asked for a seriously alcoholic drink to warm me up. I was told that it was too late and that the bar and kitchen were closed. The girl on the other end of the phone, wanting to be helpful, suggested that the only thing I could do was to draw a hot bath, and make myself a cup of hot tea or coffee, which was sitting, waiting to be used, courtesy of the management!

Waking up the next day I decided that Chicago was looking like winter wonderland, but that if possible next time I would like to come back in the spring, but never again in the winter!

Talking about winter weather, New York is not void of strange weather conditions either. After living there for a few years, and enduring the awfully hot and unpleasantly humid summers, I always dreaded winters. (I still do). In Manhattan I decided, all or almost all snowstorms occurred over weekends.

However, New Yorkers are very resourceful and snow, however deep, does not stop them from going out to enjoy their weekends.

Even more important than that is to get to work on Monday morning. If there are no buses because of the snow, and very few taxis, they take their skis out of their mothballs, and ski down on Fifth Avenue! The picture is really something to behold – in their colourful ski clothes and with their attaché case hanging somewhere off their jacket button, off they go!

There was one particular morning, after the almost traditional Sunday snow fall, I was lucky enough to have a cab which had to take me down Fifth Avenue, from the vicinity of 89th Street, all the way to 36th Street. I noticed something very strange, and it took me a few seconds to realise that on my right, Central Park looked glorious and was covered with virgin white snow. However, the road itself was very wet, and yet on my left the pavement in front of those famous apartment buildings was bone dry, with not one snowflake on it! I always regretted not having a camera on that beautiful snowy Monday morning!

I have mentioned the wonderful delicacy, potato skin with melted cheese before. Let me tell you about my interest in good food.

When people realised that I was a Hungarian, they used to ask two questions: "Do I cook goulash every day?" and "Do I know the Gabor 'Girls?"

My answer to both questions was "No". I only knew the Mother of the 'Gabors', and I only cook goulash once in a blue moon, or when non-Hungarian friends ask me to, whichever comes more seldom!

Well, I certainly moved to the right place to learn a lot about good food from various parts of the world when I went to live to New York. Luckily not all Americans eat burgers and French fries – although they can be excellent too, if they are well made and not eaten too often. I was lucky enough to make friends who originated from various countries, who were good cooks, and who also took the trouble to make wonderful meals for their friends.

The trend was to buy half prepared dishes, because it was so quick after a day's work, but a certain 'craze' was developed by people interested in good food and they did invite you for really interesting meals. Let me tell you about one of my most memorable 'culinary' experiences.

We went to see Zeffirelli's Traviata, on a Saturday afternoon, in the little cinema, opposite the Bergdorf Goodman department store. The cinema was called Paris and it was always showing foreign films. After having watched the film twice, we walked up just a few steps on 58th Street, and then down to the basement to a Pakistani restaurant, which had opened not long before.

The Pakistani restaurant was called Shezan. The place was very elegant, simple, with modern décor, in excellent taste, and I fell for it immediately. Even the glasses were perfect in my eyes. But the food! I have eaten many different Indian meals, but this was something different. I must have looked very pleased, because the manageress of the restaurant asked me how I had liked the wonderful chicken in tandoori style, with rice cooked to perfection and the Naan bread just out of the oven. Not to mention the special rice pudding covered with a thin silver topping, which I found out afterwards, was actually made with silver.

This lovely lady, who wore a beautiful sari, took me to see the kitchen, which I enjoyed no end. My hostess was Mrs. Maisy Krikliwy, from Pakistan. She told me that she was the widow of a white Prussian officer who in the Colonial Service worked very close with Lord Mountbatten. Maisy started to come up to my apartment when I had people I thought she would like to meet. She always brought the rice pudding with the silver top. At that time there was a Shezan restaurant in London too, and when Maisy heard I was again coming to Britain, she phoned to tell them that I was coming to eat there and I received VIP treatment, which meant that the food was even better, if that was possible.

Through Maisy I met a wonderfully handsome Pakistani who was by this time the manager of a small chain of hotels in Washington DC. He became even more interesting when I learned that he was married to a blonde blue-eyed American girl from the Pennsylvania Amish country.

When I first met her I asked her what her family had thought of her marrying a Pakistani person. She told me that they had met in University and fell in love. It was obvious to both of them that they were made for each other, but that didn't make it better for the very traditional Amish society, which does not accept outsiders. There was a drift and only after she had given birth to her three beautiful sons was everything forgiven.

There is one more little anecdote I feel I must tell you about some people who lived in the same building as I.

The husband was a real smart lawyer (at least he thought he was), his wife was in some business of her own, and they had two smallish children – so they made the 'Ideal American Family'. The story is that on a very rainy winter's evening she was visiting some friends in Lower Manhattan and was ready to go home. She apparently tried to call for a taxi and naturally because of the rain there was none available in Lower Manhattan. She phoned her smart lawyer husband, who I am sure, earlier in the day had closed or at least almost closed a big 'deal', asking him to get a taxi at our building (because in Uptown it was easier) and to go and get her. He did get a taxi, went to the address where she was waiting for him and went up to the apartment of her friend to get his wife. They went downstairs, she thinking that the taxi would be waiting for them. Of course it was not there. When she asked her husband where the taxi was, he told her that he had paid him and let him go!

When the doorman, not Eric of course, but one of the others, told us this story I wondered just how smart this lawyer really was and what sort of deals did he close on that wet day in New York city!

CHAPTER SEVENTEEN

~ Culture in New York ~

Of course, as I mentioned before, I have this urgent need to see plays too.

One of the biggest joys during my New York life was to be able to see everything I wanted to see in the theatre. I had the pleasure of seeing Katherine Hepburn twice and Jack Lemmon twice. I also saw Henry Fonda in his 'One Man Show' playing the life of Clarence Darrow, just to mention a few.

I was also lucky enough to see some of the best British actors on stage on Broadway. There were John Guilgud and Ralph Richardson together, twice; Richard Burton in Camelot, and Anthony Hopkins in Equis. I also saw Tom Conti in 'Whose Life Is It Anyway?', Diana Rigg, David Jacobi and many others. I felt very British seeing those wonderful actors on stage while living in New York.

I also followed beautiful Rosemary Harris around for years, and wherever she played I went to see her. I saw Ian McKellan with Peter Firth in Amadeus, and I also saw Robert Lindsay making his name on Broadway in 'Me & My Girl'. Now, back in Britain, I try to go to see him in whatever theatre he is playing.

One of the saddest evenings in a theatre for me was the last time Yul Brynner came to Broadway to do 'The King & I'. Tickets were difficult to get because everybody who liked this charismatic actor – and there were many who did – wanted to see him for the last time. If you didn't know how very ill he was, you would not have noticed. He acted and sang and danced exactly as he did so many years earlier when he was young, and before his terrible illness so cruelly attacked him. His courage and determination to do it once more was very, very impressive. His audiences showed their appreciation by the longest standing ovations. Every evening was the same; people standing, all the women crying and I had the feeling most of the men too. Those who saw him knew that no other actor would ever be able to 'take over' the role he had created about the cruel king, who was also so loveable that one could not fail to fall in love with him.

Coco Chanel, the famous fashion designer died in the early seventies and a play went on stage very soon after based on her life. Katherine Hepburn was to play the part of this very creative individual who certainly changed the way women dress. Even after all these years many of the things she made are still being copied. Her sling-back shoes, her quilted handbags made in the late '20's or early '30's are still high fashion.

I knew immediately that I had to see Coco's story, played by the legendary Miss Hepburn. We had the first two seats on the right hand side. We were early and I started to do what I loved doing – watching people walk in to see what they were wearing.

Well, I was sort of hanging out of my seat, looking back, careful not to miss any well-dressed person, when I noticed a pair of very narrow, elegant turquoise satin court shoes, walking towards me. I looked up and the fringes of a perfectly matching mohair shawl were hanging down, partially covering the longish dress, made out of the same satin as the shoes. I thought she must be very 'brave', because she obviously liked to dress up, and mohair shawls were not in fashion that season. I looked up and it was no other than the famous Duchess of Windsor, formerly Mrs. Wallis Simpson.

On her left was the very frail-looking Duke, his right arm on the arm of the Duchess, with his left hand leaning on a cane. He was dressed in a beautiful light grey double-breasted suit and looked very elegant himself. He reminded me of those finely carved ivory Chinese figures of old men – he was pale and quite beautiful, with a very kind face. The Duchess's face was stern, hard and unfriendly-looking. They were seated in the first two seats on the other side of the aisle, two rows closer to the stage than we were. In fact they were so near to us I could almost touch them. I got terribly excited and told Paul that they were obviously going to pass us on the way out. I said that I would stop the Duke and tell him that I lived in Cardiff and how the people there still remembered him when he was the Prince of Wales, and how many of them still loved him.

People in the theatre noticed that this very famous couple was there but nobody bothered them – New Yorkers are used to seeing famous people and knew how to behave. By the time the first intermission came, almost everybody must have been aware of their presence, but they let them leave without interference. It was only as they were walking back to their seats for the second half, that everyone stood up giving them a standing ovation!

Well, I don't know if you will believe this, the Duke stopped at one person to say hello, and that person was me! Unfortunately I did not remember to tell him about Cardiff, I did not even remember his title and instead of calling him "Your Royal Highness", I called him Sir!

He held my hand, and asked me how I liked the play. I said I felt very privileged to meet him – we wished each other all the best, and the most exciting few minutes of my life came to an end! The Duke died a short period later, but the memory has lived with me ever since.

One of the really outstanding events for me was to be invited to the newly opened Kennedy Centre in beautiful Washington DC. We were to participate in a Fashion Show in order to raise money for charity. We all stayed in the infamous Watergate Hotel, which of course is very luxurious. After the show there was an auction for the pieces of art and crafts we were asked earlier on to make. For some reason the organisers took it for granted that all designers must be able to 'make' something that had nothing to do with what they design for their collections. I had made a tapestry wall hanging, which made a nice little sum of money for the charity and was bought by a very famous lady who was the head of one of the biggest Washington newspapers. It was very exciting to watch the auctioneer as he went higher and higher, trying to make more and more money, in this case for charity. Afterwards there was a dinner in the main ballroom of the Centre, which as they say in these days, was the 'Mother of all dinners!' I still look at the gold (looking) plaque with my name on it. I have really collected some fantastic memories, haven't I?

Vera Bacall also recommended me to the multi-talented Rita Moreno, the star of West Side Story. She was a natural, funny, very nice and friendly woman. Her favourite garment was the, in those days, very fashionable knitted one-piece jumpsuit. We made several of them for her. She used to come up in the lunch hour and sit with the girls and myself at the big table in the workshop to eat food with us. They loved her, not only because she certainly was one out of the two stars they ever had the chance to eat with, but because being Puerto Rican she spoke with them in Spanish. She brought her husband Dr. Lenny Gordon up once; we made friends and they came to me to the apartment for dinner. Lenny really liked my cooking.

Another lovely star was the British born Celeste Holm. We made several outfits for her for a play and also for herself.

Anyway, back to my friend Vera Bacall. One day Vera told me that she wanted me to meet a very old friend of hers; an elderly Russian lady who's name was Gilda Silberstein. I met this little woman who was wearing a black coat, a babushka on her head and with a small satchel hanging on her left arm. Her name, Gilda, was very unfortunate, because that name reminded me of the beautiful Rita Hayworth, who played Gilda in the film many years before. Anyway, the reason for Vera introducing me to Gilda was that she knew of my love for the theatre, and Gilda could get tickets for shows and plays that were sold out, etc.

You see Gilda's late husband had been the physician for the Metropolitan Opera House and Carnegie Hall (the very famous concert house), for years. However, even though Dr Silberstein had died many years before I met her, she still managed to phone the box office and ask for two tickets for an opera (for instance), which was the 'hottest ticket in town'.

She would phone, and she would be told that they sold out, to which this little plain, unassuming lady would say:

"Darling (everybody was darling) you seem to forget what my husband did for the theatre" (twenty years before). In order to get rid of her, they would somehow manage to find two tickets; if they really did not have any available they would give her two passes!

However, going in to the Auditorium with passes was not pleasant. We had to wait for the curtain to go up, and the lights to go down. Some little time later one of the ushers would take us to two empty seats. Once or twice we actually sat on chairs, like the ushers did during the performance.

In most cases we had wonderful seats and it took me a long time to find out why. You see only people with money would let their tickets just go, if for some reason they could not get to the theatre. Those people, who worked hard for the price of the ticket, would try to make it to the theatre even if they were half dead, because it was too expensive to stay home and not use it. And if they really couldn't make it, they would either sell or even give the tickets to someone else to use. I also learned later that the little bag on Gilda's left arm contained a box of candies, or chocolates for the nice person who seated us!

While I sometimes found it demeaning to stand in the darkened theatre waiting to be seated, let me tell you some of the super – mega – stars I saw on stage, and some of them I even met as a result of this little woman's talent for conniving

I had heard Pavarotti on two occasions and Gilda actually managed to get a security clearance for the two of us to go backstage to meet him. He is larger than life; he filled his dressing room and is a very impressive figure indeed.

Gilda, with the most charming voice said,"Luciano, darling, this is Mady, who is in love with you" (I was not)!

Pavarotti, holding my hand in his very large hand said: "That is a mistake, because I am married".

I said, "That does not matter".

He replied, "Oh, but I have a very jealous Italian wife."

Meeting this wonderful artist was very exciting, I must admit. During my few years of friendship with Gilda I met stars like Itzak Perlman, who, in spite of his very tragic disability is charming, smiling, kind and friendly. He played in the concert with Ashkenazy, who is a totally different man, being a very serious and quiet person.

I managed to see Rudy Nureyev in two ballets. The first time he was magic and I felt sorry for the ballerina dancing with him, because his stage presence was so overwhelming that you could not look at anyone else. Unfortunately, when I saw him the second time, he was a shadow of his former self, who for years had dominated the stage.

I saw Michael Barisnykov twice, he was a fantastic dancer too, totally different from Nureyev. I also saw Joan Sutherland in the opera that she made more famous than it was before Lucia Di Lammermor. She was a fantastic singer, one of the greatest ever. I saw Placido Domingo, who was – and still is – not only a fantastic tenor, but also very attractive. It was always easy to believe that the leading lady could fall in love with him in the role he portrayed on stage.

I must admit however, that I managed to see many wonderful performances only with the help of Gilda; shows that I would not have been able to see.

Gilda was a timid little lady, without a sense of humour. Let me tell you about an evening when she got tickets for us for a concert, taking place in Carnegie Hall. It was a bitterly cold Saturday evening, and after the performance we took her to the Russian Tearoom, which is next door to Carnegie Hall.

I had made a reservation for three and the place was totally full. We were shown to a corner table, which normally seated two, and we were sitting in a very cosy manner. A few minutes later Warren Beatty walked in with a young woman and their table was just a few inches away from ours. (The Russian Tearoom was famous for using every square inch and it was always wonderful to watch the waiters walking sideways between the tables, because the place was so full.) Well, Mr Beatty, who looked very attractive wearing an expensive sheepskin coat, stood up, and announced to his companion that he is going to the men's room.

I said to Gilda and Paul, "I am very disappointed because I did not know that famous movie stars like Warren Beatty do 'that kind of thing'!"

Gilda turned to me, with a very serious expression and said: "Darling, I have been married to a medical doctor for forty-five years. I know quite a bit about medicine and I have to tell you that everybody has to go to the toilet!"

That was the time that I decided never to try to be funny in front of Gilda!

I would not swap these wonderful experiences for anything.

CHAPTER EIGHTEEN

~ Business as usual ~

If I remember correctly, it was the middle of the seventies when many Russian Jews were allowed to leave the Soviet Union. They came to the United States because of the belief that the New York streets were full of dollar bills and all you had to do was bend down and pick them up. This was the reason that many of these people settled in the Big Apple.

This was also one of the times when I needed more machine knitters, and so I advertised. Several of these Russian women applied and came for appointments. Some looked promising and so we gave them wool and a pattern to make a sample. We also mentioned the going rate, which was not at all bad.

To my biggest surprise, three of them returned with the sample that they had made, which was not only damp, but also almost wet. I immediately knew what they had done (and why). However, I asked them why they made the garment wet. After their various attempts to give me some explanation, I had to tell them that they were not in the glorious Soviet Union any longer and they didn't have to do things like that. This was because we paid proper prices for all their work. If you remember, earlier on I told you that the only way – back in Hungary – we could make a little extra money was to make our knitted pieces damp, to be able to weigh in more on delivery. These poor women, who still did not know any better, had tried to do the same. The sad part of all this was that they had not yet had the time to learn to trust anybody. Not one of them came back for more work.

Funnily enough I was trusted by women from all different countries and religions, but not by Jewish women who were less fortunate than I was. After all, I had already spent 16-18 years out of the hell of Comrade Stalin and the rest of those wonderful leaders, who still, this late in the day, completely disregarded human needs.

Talking about all those women – most of them were really nice – with whom I was working quite happily, I must tell you what a little workshop like mine was really like. In busy times we were maybe 16-17 of us, including me – getting together every morning at 8am and working until 4pm. We had coffee and lunch together on our long table and had little trouble, other than the unfortunate deep-rooted hatred of different nationalities.

Let me explain: Say that the little group consisted of one girl from Chile, Luisa, who felt that amongst all South and Central Americans she was the most superior, and so looked down on all the others.

There was our fantastic knitter, the Argentinean Estella, who did not really like people who came from a 'lesser country' than hers, but really hated Nelly, also from Chile, but not as racist as the others.

I have to tell you something funny that happened during the public transport strike, which, while it did last several weeks did not stop people getting into Manhattan to work every day. At this time, my super Hungarian dressmaker, Angela's husband, drove a limousine for his living. His name was Leslie and he was a good friend. We made a deal with him, and he, starting at 6 am, picked up all my ladies who lived in the Bronx, Queens and all over, and transported them to 36th Street, where our workplace was.

On one of these mornings Leslie wanted to tell me "something funny". He told me, that Estella, the Argentinean, had offered him $1,000 cash if he pushed Nelly, the Chilean – into the East River.

I told him that the only thing that was funny was that he thought Estella was joking. I assured him that she was totally serious!

So about the other ladies: The Ecuadorians did not like the ones from Paraguay – although there was a little love affair going on between one male and one female from those two little countries. Does it mean, 'love conquers all' even if the serious duty is to hate the person who happens to come from the country next to yours?

We had two girls from Peru and they were also different from the others, because while the others only hated the ones who were "immediately under" themselves, these poor Peruvians were hated by all the others. This hatred became so strong that we actually had to let them go in order to save them from – possibly – getting seriously hurt or even killed.

I sometime said to these ladies, "We Europeans (an Italian lady, one from France but born in Spain – a wonderful friend, we still visit each other after all these years, and two super women from Portugal, etc.) – We all come from different countries and we are quite happily working together". However, it did not change the hatred between the South and Central Americans.

It was also at this time that I had a telephone call from one of the women whom I had known back in Budapest and who lived in Queens with her third husband. Her name was Magda and I was surprised to hear from her as we were not close friends and did not talk on the telephone often. When she told me the reason for her call I had a terrible shock. Let me tell you about this sad telephone conversation.

There were two sisters living in Kispest with their loving parents and they were known as the 'Inseparable Sigfried Sisters' – Liz and Roz. Their father was a jeweller and watchmaker and had a good small business on the High Street. The Sigfried parents did not come back from deportation. The two sisters survived and I am sure, hand in hand, they helped and supported one another throughout their ordeal. After their return Liz, who was a qualified jeweller and watchmaker like her father, started a little business and made a reasonable living. Roz, the younger one, married a textile chemist soon after the war. He had a good job and they had a beautiful daughter, Judy. Liz got married later and had a boy, Gabor. Both marriages got into trouble; both 'the Inseparable Sigfrieds' divorced and, like old times, they supported one another and their children. Liz lived in her own house in a side street off the main road in Kispest. It was a typical Hungarian suburban house with a large gate that opened into an enclosed yard. Entry to the house was through the gate, which was locked, and then through the yard. The house was a one-level construction level with the street, which had big windows through which you could talk to passers-by.

A voice calling her name awakened Liz very early one Sunday morning. She opened her bedroom window and saw her neighbour's teenage daughter being chased by her boyfriend who had a revolver in his hand. Without hesitating, Liz ran out to the yard, opened the gate, let the girl in and pushed her to safety. But before she had a chance to close the gate, the boy shot her three times in the stomach. Roz was called and Liz was taken to hospital where she died a day or so later. Poor Roz fell apart; they had been together all their lives – before, during and after their deportation. They really were the closest, most loving sisters I ever knew. If someone had asked one of them to die for the other, there would have been no hesitation. Those two lovely, decent, devoted sisters, loved by many friends had survived so much misery together, only to be parted by murder because Liz had been kind enough to help someone. Roz became obsessed with trying to see justice done. It was a mystery how the boy had managed to get hold of a firearm in a country where ordinary people had no access to such things. But he was never convicted and Roz became more and more depressed and even the love of her daughter Judy, and her family could not help her. She told me on the odd days I spent with her during my visits to Budapest that her nightmares from the camps were returning constantly and that she could not get over Liz's death. She kept on saying that she should have been the one to be murdered and not Liz, because Liz was always the stronger one.

On my last meeting with them both, they took me to dinner to the newly opened fabulous Hilton Hotel in Buda. Our table was by the window overlooking the Danube, with wonderful views of the beautiful Pest part of Budapest. During dinner I asked them to visit me in New York where I lived at that time. Liz said to Roz, "I can't go now because of the shop, but why don't you go with Mady".

"You know I never go anywhere without you, Liz" Roz said.

I was sitting with Roz many years after Liz's death during a visit to Budapest. We were having coffee and delicious cakes in the Viennese Café in the Forum Hotel in Budapest and I asked her again to come and stay with me, but this time to South Wales.

"I can give you work, I live in my cottage alone, and there is plenty of room, plenty to do, we could get on well together. I can even pay you", I said. She was a clever knitter and finisher, and I had a good business then, whereas I knew she was terribly worried about her own business in Budapest where people had very little money to buy anything. She used every excuse in the book to turn down my invitation.

Four weeks later I had a phone call to say that Roz had died. My first question was "Was it suicide?"

Tragically it was. She had visited Judith, her husband and the children on the Sunday before her death – as she always did – measured them all for sweaters for Christmas and then she'd gone home and killed herself. Judith found her beloved mother the next day, dead in the bathtub.

Was it the aftermath of her beloved sister's death, was it the realisation that 'the other half of her' was no longer, or was it just the recurring nightmares of our past that took her to this desperate decision? Loving her family as she did, I felt that this was not my wonderful friend Roz who has committed this terrible crime against those who loved her exquisitely. This must have been a fatal move of some person whom we obviously did not really know.

I have visited Washington DC several times. The Smithsonian Institute, all its buildings are the most wonderful museums. To see all they contain would probably take years.

Walking in George Town and having a meal there is good fun. The City itself is very beautiful, a real representative of the USA.

The saddest place, however majestic is Arlington Cemetery, with its rows of identical graves, the final resting places of all those wonderful young men and women who died during different wars. Of course the Kennedy's grave is something you will never forget, once you have seen it. I have a question here too. Why were those two brothers assassinated? Why do people murder each other?

CHAPTER NINETEEN

~ Celebrities and Personalities ~

I went to Miami Beach to do a show in a shop, and went into the Elizabeth Arden Salon. It was here that I met Shirley Bassey, for whom we had made one or two outfits. She was a very natural, kind and nice person. When I mentioned to her that I was friendly with her ex-physical education teacher, (Dot) from the Splott Secondary Modern School in Cardiff, she immediately said: "Oh yes, Miss Whiston, do give her my regards".

She invited me to her show in the famous 'Fontainbleu Hotel'. She was great, as usual.

One of my 'trunk show' trips took me to Oklahoma City. Before I went there, the only thing I knew about the place was that one of my most favourite musicals was named after it. When I arrived, I was shown around the town by the very nice people for whom I was going to do the show.

It was interesting for me to see that very close to the main office building, I think City Hall, there was oil pumping out through two (one on either side) of those huge contraptions that were made for this purpose.

The city itself reminded me of the wonderful film, which I learned was back in Britain in its original shape as a stage musical. It was most welcomed by the British audiences when it arrived on the London stage after the war, as Britain was still suffering from the aftermath of those terrible years.

It was also during these years that my daughter Ildi finished at Art College and graduated as a textile designer. She, very wisely, went for a teacher's degree as well. Since then she has been teaching maladjusted children, as well as children with learning difficulties due to terrible problems in their homes.

During one of my trips to Los Angeles, I was installed in the wonderful Beverly Wiltshire Hotel, on Wiltshire Boulevard.

Here was I, this very small person from Budapest and Cardiff, via Auschwitz and Belsen, staying just a few floors below the apartment of the already famous star, Warren Beatty. If that made me feel fantastic, and it sure did, can you imagine how I felt when some people took me out for dinner to the then very 'in' restaurant, called 'Chasens'. That was a sensation on its own, but being introduced to the positively gorgeous Dean Martin was almost too much! He was tanned, handsome, and very, very sexy. He held my hand for – it must have been several seconds – and I was in heaven. I knew I would never be the same again!

People always say that nobody ever walks in Southern California; they always take the "Caddy" (if the person was more 'posh', it was a Mercedes Benz, and always white) everywhere. Well, there was one star, who did walk and that was David Jansen, star of the "Fugitive". I saw him several times and he was an elegant, handsome man. Later, on somebody's recommendation, his beautiful wife, Danny, formerly Mrs. Buddy Greco became a customer. One of the outfits we made for her was a gold Lurex; fine knitted evening pants outfit. I still look at her photograph and remember her telling me, that after her husband's untimely, sudden death at a tragically early age, how terribly she was missing him.

I also had the pleasure of meeting Mrs Jimmy Duranty. I was talking with her for a long time and she still did not mention her very much beloved, very talented, funny husband. She told me that she only mentioned him if someone asked about him.

As I was measuring this very nice woman, she pointed out to me, that I would have to take two different measurements for her arms and legs, because, due to cancer surgery, one arm and one thigh were thicker than the other. I remember thinking that there is this lovely woman, adored by the very funny and famous Jimmy Duranty, who should be in seventh heaven, in a very good marriage, but she had to go through this terrible ordeal too. Is it really true, that all nice people have to have some tragedy in their lives?

Back in New York, I don't remember the exact year, the wonderful musical; "My Fair Lady" was making a 'come back'. The classical role of Professor Henry Higgins was again played by the superb Rex Harrison. Of course I wanted to see it and I was asked by the young woman, who played Elisa, to chaperon her teenage daughter to the opening night. (My daughter knew her from London and, because I was in New York, they asked me.) I went with the greatest of pleasure, not only because I wanted to see it again but also because we were to go back stage and I was hoping to meet "Sexy Rexy"! Mr Harrison must have been in his late seventies, still stunning and indeed very sexy. When I told him how very nervous I was to meet him, he said to me, "real 'Hunkies' don't get nervous. Look at 'Laszlo' the Hungarian in the play". Meeting Mr Harrison was something I will never forget either.

Also among my special private customers there was a lady who was tiny in stature, but her personality and intellect was very big. She was married to Samuel Newhouse, also a tiny person, and the head of the famous Coude Nast Publications. They owned many of the most important magazines – the Company is still in business.

Mrs Newhouse, Mitzi, became a very much-loved customer, who appreciated made-to-measure things, being so petite; it was difficult for her to get good clothes. Also, she had very good taste and liked the idea of having things designed for her. She must have liked me, because she arrived many times with little gifts. One day she appeared with a bottle of perfume, the most expensive scent at that time: "Joy" by Jean Patou. I felt very special, when I put a little drop behind my ears.

This all happened many years ago, but on my visits to New York, I am always reminded of Mr and Mrs Newhouse, because of their generous donations to the city as well as to many charities. As you walk in towards the Metropolitan Opera, on the Lincoln Centre, on the left of the Opera building, there is a theatre called the "Mitzi Newhouse Theatre", donated by this wonderful couple. The theatre is a fitting memory to them. Lincoln Centre is a very special place with the Opera, with all the interesting Chagall frescos, the Philharmonic Hall and the City Opera. These are all important; maybe the most important parts of International Culture. I had my opera season ticket on the same day as the Newhouses and they invited me to the VIP lounge on a few occasions. This was the kind of treat that I loved, being a people watcher and a stargazer. Knowing Mr and Mrs Newhouse was one of the high lights of my being in my little business in the Big Apple.

I also got to know a lady at this time, who was a fashion writer, publishing a paper called "Fashion Newsletter". Her name was Leona Bowman. Her nice husband was the owner of one of the best Art Galleries in Manhattan. There was a super story about her and I am going to tell it to you, but first I have to tell you the background. The Fashion designing family "Fendi" was becoming really famous with their first fantastically successful handbag, which was made out of very narrow strips of leather and woven together. Because it became so popular, naturally many bag manufacturers copied it very quickly. One of these manufacturers was a New York firm, by the name of Maurice Moskowitz.

Well, now comes the story about Leona Bowman. Leona and her husband were in Paris for Fashion Week and had the good taste to stay in the Paris Ritz. One morning a very well dressed Italian male (aren't they all well dressed?) got into the lift, turned to Leona who had one of those beautiful woven leather bags hanging off her left shoulder and said "Fendi?" Leona in very good humour answered: "No unfortunately only Maurice Moskowitz".

I also had a telephone call from a woman one day who told me that the First Lady, Mrs. Richard Nixon had seen my work in some shop and wanted me to make some things for her, and could I meet her (Mrs. Nixon) in the Waldorf Astoria Towers. What a question! Could I meet Mrs. Nixon? If I had to walk to the Waldorf in the middle of a very cold, wet, snowy horrible night, I would meet her!

Pat Nixon was a lovely, quiet friendly all-American woman. She was a perfect size 10 US, which means that in GB (British size) she was very small, a size 12. She was blond, wearing very little make-up, and was a conservative dresser with very good taste. She ordered several outfits, both day and eveningwear. The day she received her parcel her cheque was in the mail. I mention this because several VIP ladies did not believe in paying their bills, saying – like Madame Gabor did a few years before

– "It is a great honour for you to work for us, dear!" The last time I met Mrs Nixon was on the memorable Friday, in the lunch hour on the day the Mr Nixon was about to introduce his new Vice President, Jerry Ford. It was after the departure of Mr. Spiro Agnew, the previous Vice President. I knew that Mrs Nixon had to fly to Washington DC after our fitting, in a helicopter, and she hated it. I took a long stem red rose for her, and she said as she accepted it that it would make her journey less miserable.

I said, "God bless, Mrs Nixon", to which she replied, "Mady, dear, do you think He will?"

I will always remember her tear-filled eyes as she held my hand in hers for a few seconds. She wore a suit we had made for her for the last important speech Mr Nixon delivered before he had to depart in total disgrace. Mrs Nixon made only one big mistake in my estimation, and that was to have married Richard Nixon.

I still have two photographs dedicated to me, and also a Christmas card from the White House from 'The President and Mrs Nixon'.

One of the most interesting and creative people I ever met, not only in New York, but anywhere I have ever been, was a tiny person but tiny only in stature. In personality and creativity Clara Josephs was a giant. Clara was a widow by the time I met her. She was Vera Bacall's best and oldest friend. Vera lovingly called her 'Zuleika'.

Clara was a wonderful artist and I could never understand why she was not famous. She did tell me once, when I asked her why she does not show her paintings, why she only paints for herself. She told me that she used to take commissions, but when someone wanted to order a painting to match their sofa she was so upset about the bad taste of people that she just gave up. I never found out if this was serious or was she just giving me a reply.

Clara lived in one of the old, very prestigious apartment buildings on Central Park West. The apartment was one of those converted ones, which in the old times used to be just one on each floor, and as real estate became more and more expensive; these places were converted into two, maybe three smaller units. Clara had an unusual place because the conversion gave her two bedrooms and three bathrooms. One of the bathrooms became the 'Picasso' bathroom.

This bathroom had a freestanding Victorian tub. The tub had the figure of a naked female lying full length; she had to put her feet (the lady's feet) vertically up on the foot of the bathtub! If this was not funny enough, she painted a big yellow bird on the left shoulder of the reclining female! I asked her how she managed to do this and she told me that she had to get into the tub and drew around her body!

The living room, the hall and the whole apartment was full of interesting pieces of art and crafts, which all represented her excellent taste and eccentricity.

Her own paintings were strong and powerful. The one that I admired most was a large oil painting with a sort of red waterfall coming down from some rocks. She painted this after the assassination of President Kennedy and the red waterfall was symbolising Kennedy's blood.

Clara showed me the beginning of her 'autobiography'. This was the first of three large oils. She started to tell of her life story in the attic of her parents house, with some old pieces of furniture, bits of old toys, even a beautiful painted rocking horse. Clara told me that she couldn't write her life story, so she painted it instead.

I did see all three paintings and I was convinced that she could have become famous even at the latter stage of her life. All she wanted it for was to leave it for her two beloved children and the two grandchildren.

In between painting these strong oils Clara made some beautifully delicate collages, tiny fine pieces of paper that she cut out of magazines and put them together. This was to create these collages, all which told a different story. I am privileged to have several of these and every time I look at them they remind me of my wonderful friend, Clara. She wore many of my 'knits', which was a great compliment to me.

I not only loved her but I also learned a lot from her. We used to go to Museums and Galleries together and I had the very best teacher. Clara was also a music and opera lover, so we did not find it difficult to spend time together.

Clara's daughter Harriett is a fine pianist and when she was giving concerts I used to go with Clara to listen to her playing.

Clara was one of the most beloved friends I ever had and when I left her and came back to Britain, I not only missed her, but also felt guilty about leaving her.

During the '70's and early 80's I was working with an Italian man who helped me to see new yarns developed in that wonderful, creative country of his. I in those years used to go to Italy, first to beautiful Florence, then to Milan to the fashion shows. My Italian 'agent' met me on a few of these trips and took me to yarn factories to see the new developments. One of these trips took us to a small industrial town called Prato, I think, just a few miles out of Florence. As he was driving me around I asked him to tell me about this small town, which I had to admit was not nearly as picturesque as most others in beautiful Italy. He told me that his family had been living there for many generations and they were very happy, until after the Second World War, the 'emigrants' arrived. Because I could not imagine why anyone would want to immigrate to a place like that I did ask who the emigrants were. He replied, "Well, the ones from the South".

I asked him, "The south of what?"

His totally shocking reply (to me) was, "From the south of Italy, of course".

He told me, after I asked him why the southern Italians were considered 'foreigners', that the crime rate had gone up drastically since they had 'invaded' the northern part of their own country. He also said that his own parents felt they could not go to their 'own' church any more and that morals were down, etc.

I still did not understand this obviously terrible racism and asked how they could tell from the news in the papers and the television that these crimes were being committed by the 'newcomers'? He informed me that even their names were different from the names of those people in the north of Italy.

I think I came away from that meeting with an otherwise nice man feeling that the world has not got a chance. I hope I am wrong.

CHAPTER TWENTY

~ Travelling for Holidays ~

Living and working in New York means that you are working harder than ever before. If you have a 'nine to five' job you might be able to put everything down at five, and by the time you get home hope to forget all about it, but working for yourself is a different proposition altogether. You don't put a project down, you try to finish it and by the time you get home you are so tired that you forget how you actually got home!

I am mentioning this because I always felt that I had to justify to myself I needed a holiday, or did I just want one? In either case I travelled more than I could afford and I am so glad that I did. Travelling is one of the wonderful things in life (for me at least).

After moving to New York I started to learn to like going to the 'Islands'. New Yorkers go 'down South' like the Torontonians like to go 'up North'. The nearest island is beautiful Bermuda, and I managed to learn to enjoy it very quickly! I find it much easier to get used to nice things rather than bad things. I am almost sure that most people do too.

But back to Bermuda: if you have not been yet and you can afford to, please do not hesitate – go! It is wonderful; it is full of hibiscus, which grows wild in various shades of pink and is full of the perfume of that beautiful flower.

Bermuda is very clean – as a matter of fact as the plane approaches the island one can see the corals at the bottom of the ocean. The people are wonderful and the tax-free shopping is great! I have to mention here that being a Hungarian I am sort of proud of the beautiful porcelain pottery they are making 'back home'. It is called 'Herend' and is by now a collector's item. Every piece is hand painted and there are some truly nice pieces.

Well, on one of my first visits to Bermuda, walking on Front Street in the capital of the Island Hamilton, my curiosity ushered me into a shop called "Bluck's", selling porcelain, crystal and other beautiful and expensive things. I don't remember exactly but I think the shop is over 200 years old, and is also British. To my biggest surprise I found the largest selection of 'Herend' that I have ever seen. I started to talk to the manageress and she actually confirmed that they are the largest stockists of Hungarian china. I went into Bluck's every time I went to Bermuda, and by this time I developed a taste for another, even more beautiful china than 'Herend'. It comes from Denmark and it is made in the famous Royal Copenhagen Porcelain factory. It is called 'Flora Danica' and is a delicate shade of off-white, with a fine gold edge. Every piece is painted with a different flower and it takes your breath away.

Well, I was in Bluck's on one of my visits – I was actually buying something, but had to wait for the lady, who by now recognised me, because she was making up the bill for a small but important looking Japanese gentleman. After receiving his bill he picked up his attaché case from the floor, and in front of me, counted out very close to $35,000 in cash! He took his receipt and left the store. I was in a state of shock and the nice lady told me that the gentleman had purchased a complete set of 12, dinner, coffee and all for his only daughter who was just getting married! I said that I would not like to be living in a household where that china would be used. I think one dinner plate cost over $100. Can you imagine dropping one?

We stayed in various hotels on that magic island, and I took Ildi there once or twice and loved it every time.

Travelling from New York as I mentioned before takes you to different destinations, and one tries to go in the winter because it is so awful. Visiting the various islands is 'the thing to do'. I decided to take Ildi to South America for her 21st birthday. I wish that I hadn't.

First stop was the truly magnificent city of Rio de Janeiro. Beautiful for the 'have's', absolutely awful for the 'have not's'. Standing on the balcony of our hotel room, looking left to the marvellous Copacabana beach and admiring the most magnificent bodies of the young natives is really fantastic, as long as one does not look to the right. There in the very near vicinity one sees all those poor people going up to their shacks where there is no sanitation, no electricity, nothing else, only misery.

Our next stop was in Lima, Peru. Rio was paradise compared to Lima. We only had three or four days and wanted to see as much as possible, so we hired a driver – very cheap – who took us out of that terrible city to see some more pleasant places. He told us that it never rains in Lima, that he was 53 years old and had lived there all his life, and so far had only ever experienced two rainfalls in his life. Because of the lack of rain there is a fine, almost black dust covering everything, even the inside of the petals of some roses an old lady was trying to sell on the street corner. The poor walk in dust on one side of the road, but on 'millionaire's row' on the other side there is plenty of water, even for the servants to wash the 'posh' cars and water the potted plants on the rich people's rooftops.

I only then understood why the Peruvian people had grey complexions. They are not white, or black, or yellow, they are positively grey because the terrible dust settles in their pores. I got so depressed that we actually tried to leave sooner than scheduled, but could not get a flight. As much as I love travelling I hated South America. We visited Caracas as our last port of call and it was the same story – the most beautiful expensive shops in the city, the most unbearable poverty just a few yards out of it. I decided that this is the part of the world I never want to return to.

CHAPTER TWENTY-ONE

~ Epilogue ~

I keep on wanting to finish this story and have found out that it is much easier to write a little more and then another little more, rather than to close it. This is the kind of feeling actors and artists must suffer with, knowing that they should call it a day, but hang on in there a little longer.

I have looked back and remembered friends and relatives and I want people to know their stories and so I am writing about them in order that readers can see how ordinary people can be affected by an extraordinary and evil regime.

The first visit back to Hungary in 1964 was a strange experience. We looked different and the taxi driver immediately knew that we were from the west because we had decent clothes. We might have even smelled different. We certainly sounded different. Eight short years in Britain had given us a feeling of 'security' that had nothing to do with money, it had everything to do with living in a free country, with being able to talk, feel, walk, and work freely. Not only that, but of having been accepted by the British people, and knowing that in time we would become part of Great Britain.

However, this was going to be a short account of what happened to so many people (and me) at that terrible time, back in the '40s. I really wanted to tell you mostly about those lovely people whom I liked, loved and most of whom I lost. If I wrote too much about myself too, I hope you will forgive me; I wrote it as it came out of my heart.

The New York part must sound less depressing. Maybe some people (if anyone actually gets to read this) will think that the fast pace of New York, meeting all those exciting people, all that travelling and all the other nice things I had the chance of experiencing, made me forget about my 'first life'. I have not and could not ever forget those years and all the years that followed.

The year I returned to Britain was 1985 - Ildi had two beautiful children, Jess, aged 6 years, and Saskia, aged 4 ½ years. New York is very far away from London, and while it is a very exciting place for the young, getting old there is only good if your family are there as well and also if you have a lot of money. I had neither, so it was time for me to return to the UK. In any case, this was the country where people accepted us, and nobody examined us to figure out if we were legitimate refugees or only people who were looking for the chance of a better life. But is that such a crime? When someone asks me where my roots are, I can only say, they must be in Britain, because even if I had some back in the old country, the Nazis destroyed them.

It is this country where I feel that I belong. It is true that the weather is not perfect, but people are nice. It is also true that it is not easy to make money, but I have wonderful friends, a good social life and that makes up for a lot. When I put the 'pros' and 'cons' on the scale, the 'pros' win out.

Now I have three smashing grandchildren, all grown up.

Just one more thing, do you remember the 15 year-old Mady who – on the way to Sweden – told the Swedish doctor that she hopes the world has learned something from the terrors of the Second World War? Well, the seventy five year old Mady is still hoping…

Maybe my grandchildren will have a more secure, nicer world to live in by the time they are settled with their families. I can only hope so.

As I am about to finish my 'manuscript' I am determined to end it with something funny. I have some funny stories on reserve in my head but I thought nothing could be jollier than some parts of my relationship with my friend Shoi. I hope you will find it funny too.

During my years of being in the 'Fashion Business' in the 'Big Apple', I had to go to Florence to see the fashion shows – (well, I did not actually have to go, but Florence being my favourite city, and loving to travel anyway, I loved every minute of it!). As I was making the arrangements to go, one of my customers, and by this time friend, asked me if she could go with me - but before I tell you about the actual trip, let me introduce my friend whose first name was SHOI. I first thought that it was some sort of oriental name but I soon learned that she was a Jewish girl from Brooklyn.

It took me some time before I was brave enough to ask her what kind of name was 'Shoi'. She told me that her real name was Shirley, and because nobody could pronounce it properly – they called her SHOILY – she thought that Shoi would be more interesting, and also a conversation piece. So she had her name changed by Deed Poll (I think that is the right word for a legal name change)!

Shoi was a very clever woman; she was involved in some sort of 'Industrial Research', which I did not know anything about before she explained that everything in the industry has to be analysed as to how the potential customers were going to like or hate it.

She had groups of people who were called together, she then presented the new product, tested the field, made her report to the manufacturer, received huge amounts of money for her work and everybody was happy!

I had been making clothes for her for some time and it did not take my helpers and myself long to realise that she was an eccentric. You see, whenever she ordered a garment, she did not order one, she would order five or more of the identical article! She said that if she likes something, she wants to have lots of it! I remember getting her some beautiful handbags from Judith Leiber, but she wanted them in several colours!

Now I am getting on the aeroplane with her and I was sure that this was the first time in many years that she was travelling Tourist class, instead of at least Business class. You see, I made the reservations!

Shoi was always on a diet. At this particular time, she, like thousands of Americans was on the now very famous Atkins diet. She could not eat most normal things, only meats and other fats. On the 'plane I told her that Florence was not only famous for art and the jewellery on the Ponte Vecchio, but also for the wonderful food they serve to you.

I asked her why she didn't get off the diet for the few days we were going to spend in that fabulous city, and get back on it when we got to Paris, but she told me that I didn't understand the diet.

What I didn't understand was how anyone could not eat the wonderful Florentine food!

Well, the first morning I had some delicious espresso coffee, with several fresh, crisp 'paninies', the Italian bread roll which is the best in the world. Shoi had black coffee and nothing else! Two hours later she was starving and could hardly wait for lunch.

I had a small portion of salad, meat, etc., and was very happy, but by the time we got to eat at dinner she ate even more meat than at the lunchtime meal.

This went on for two days, and by the evening of that day Shoi told me she was going on a 'binge'!

She told me to take her to the little coffee shop we had been in to earlier that day and which she could never find, because, clever as she was, her sense of direction was even worse than mine, and that is saying a lot! However, I did not want to find the place, although I knew it well, so we walked round it several times. It was getting late and I was hoping that she would give up on it, but she did not. She said to me: "Why don't you admit that you cannot find it?"

Well, there was nothing I could do, so we went into the little coffee shop and I had a wonderful espresso, the best that money could buy. I told Shoi that there was nothing for her to 'binge', they had sold out almost everything, to which she pointed at some pastries and duly ordered 8, yes eight of them. After she finished them she purchased a huge chocolate Easter egg (it was Easter week) for herself to take back to the hotel.

The next morning she looked very pale and told me that "Dr. Atkins is absolutely right saying that carbohydrates make you ill!"

I replied that after devouring 8 pastries and about a kilogram of chocolate, a whole regiment of people would become ill!

We then had to take the train back to Milan in order to fly to Paris, where the fashion shows were starting the next day. To me, one of the great joys of life was to have lunch on the train between Firenze and Milano. The Italians don't ask questions, just bring one course after the other, and it is all wonderful.

My friend told me as we were getting our seats on the train that she read the 'reverse' diet by the same doctor, and now she can eat all greens and fruit, but no meat. She ordered lots of fruit and then some green salads.

The Head waiter was a bit fed up, but served her until the moment when all passengers were given wonderful coffee and Shoi asked for tea.

This was too much for the Italian, who said to the other waiter "Loco Americana". He then turned to Shoi and said: "We are only serving tea for breakfast, Signora"!

We were then waiting in the queue for our Air France aeroplane, when we were told that they had no seats for us, the reason being that Air France had overbooked. We now had 9 pieces of luggage between us – you see I had two cases, and Shoi started out from New York with three pieces, but she had purchased four more because the luggage was so beautiful in Florence…!

I tried for planes going to other places, to somehow reach Paris, but there were none that would get us there. You see when the fashion shows start the whole world wants to be there.

To cut the already long story short, the only way to get to Paris from Milan was, believe it or not, by taxi! Our porter who was standing with our nine pieces of luggage, all of a sudden remembered he had a cousin – all Italians have dozens of them and most of them are there where you need them – who was a taxi driver, not just a regular one but one who was driving a large shiny black Mercedes Benz, and he was willing to take us to Paris for $500!

Shoi thought that was too much, but I worked it out that after the refund from Air France, plus the excess luggage charge she would have to pay for her new suitcases, it was not so much! We got the price down to $400, but in the end we paid him his price because he was great. How he managed to put all that stuff into the car, we never found out!

There was something else I could never work out, which was that I was afraid that Mario (he had to be called Mario, otherwise the whole thing would not have been so perfect) only spoke Italian, I spoke English and not too much German – Hungarian does not count – Shoi spoke her American English, and yet I found out all sorts of things, not only about Sophia Loren, but even about the then Italian Government, which even Mario did not know how long they would last, because they were changing all the time!

We finally arrived in Paris just before six in the morning and were greeted by the most beautiful sight – the streets were being washed with all the reflections of the street lights, and no people anywhere.

Just a last word on this story – we met my daughter in Paris, she was there with other students from the Art College. Shoi took us out for dinner to the best steak restaurant we could find. End of her diet, even the reversed one!

Just one more thing, Shoi went to Galleries Lafayette and bought a set of bathroom scales, as she could not wait to weigh herself until she returned to New York!

CHAPTER 22

~ Returning Home ~

Returning to Britain from America after 18 years was a big step. Coming 'home' felt wonderful. Leaving my lovely friends was difficult and sad and I felt that I was doing it again. In 1956 I left my great friends in Budapest; in 1967 I did the same in Cardiff, and in 1985 I was repeating it – this time saying farewell to the nice people who were so good to me and without whom my story in New York would not have been as enjoyable as it was. I felt terrible, I felt like a traitor, I was walking away from them and because I knew that they were sorry to lose me, it hurt even more, but I had to come back to my family, to my British friends and to my adopted country.

First I thought I had to go back to Cardiff, but somehow 'going back' had a strange feeling attached to it, like going backwards? I didn't know why but I decided to settle between London – where my family lived – and Cardiff. So I picked Bath - bad choice. I opened a tiny shop on the romantic Poultney Bridge and the first year was great – tourists coming from faraway places, including New Zealand. I met a great lady, a real New Zealander by the name of Mary Aiford and we have been friends ever since. Mary is bright, clever, a true lover of the Arts, a real academic and a loving friend.

At the time of our meeting I still had my apartment in New York and we had actually met there, having lunch, going to Museums and forging a real friendship. At that time I did not know yet that Mary would be the only friend I would have from the years spent in Bath, but going back to the boutique. The second year, 1986, Mr. Reagan decided to drop a few bombs on the head of Colonel Gadafi and the tourists did not come any more – but I am going away from the subject again – a few weeks ago there was a terrible upheaval in the British airports – terrorists tried to blow up some planes with some liquid. However, British travellers did not get hysterical; they were waiting quietly for hours – days even for their plane to take off. They did not cancel their holidays; they were fantastically tolerant, patient and great. Not like those people in 1986….

Anyway, the boutique suffered, the 'Bathonians' did not come to shop; they want you to establish yourself, which takes at least three years, but it is difficult if people do not support you during those times. My workshop was busy, we were making beautiful jackets and with my gorgeous saleslady Gisele, we were selling nicely. However, the big problem for me was that hardly anyone would talk to me. I think they like to see your grandfather's pedigree, and sadly I did not have one!

So, I was very lonely and started to feel the urge to come back to Wales. I wanted to return to the part of this country where, so many years before as a refugee, people were so nice to me and my little girl. I knew that I would not be as lonely here as I was in Bath.

I started to look for a house – something we - Paul and I were getting married soon – could afford and I could love. Being a typical Taurean, born the end of April, I have an excuse for loving beautiful things, and I am also a homemaker - this is according to my horoscope.

Well, I found the house – this was the only one, after having looked at about 50 of them, which said "Welcome" as I walked in. The original cottage is old, very old, built in 1568. The house is on different levels, all up and down, just like my life! We bought it and I have loved it ever since. My life has re-started again after the miserable, lonely years in the beautiful Georgian city of Bath.

I have made many friends with the help of the wonderful vicar, Jeremy Winston, who introduced me to such nice people.

I want to mention here that after I moved in, I sent a message to the vicar inviting him for a drink. I told him that I wanted to help with whatever I can in the village, but I will not be a church-goer, because I am Jewish.

"No problem" he said. Wonderful!

It has now been 18 years, and I am still here. I love it. . It feels as if I have always been living here. I don't feel lonely (Paul passed away four years ago), I have a fabulous social life - I go to the theatre in Cardiff and Bristol, to the Opera, I am invited to people's houses, I cook for friends, love dinner parties and I am getting old like all my friends, as opposed to getting old with friends.

On my return from America, in my little flat in Bath – in the attic, 63 steps up – I started to phone all my old friends to announce that not only am I still among the living, but back home in Britain. One of the couples I phones, Val and John Gregory, John answered the phone.

I said "Hi John". He said "Mady, where are you?" So I told him, I'm back and answering his question of how I am!
I told him "OK, just getting old!" to which my lovely friend said:

"Darling, don't worry, we are all with you. Can you imagine how awful it would be to bear it all alone?"... He was right, and although he died years ago, I still remember his words of wisdom.

Back to living in South Wales again and going to the New Theatre in Cardiff. I had managed to get two tickets for "Cavalleria Rusticana and Pagliacci", on – I think – 16th April 1996. We all knew that the Welsh National Opera was celebrating its 50th birthday, but did not realise that the actual day 50 years before was the first night of the Company and the first performance 50 years before was the same "Cavalleria Rusticana and Pagliacci". It was a magical evening with Dennis O'Neil, the talented Welsh tenor singing Turiddu.

The production was magical and Mr. O'Neil was superb.

During the performance it occurred to me that April 1946, when the war was over for less than a year, the little group of Welsh people established the Opera Company, it could not have been easy, shortages on all fronts, coupons for everything, and yet they did it and it was now 50 years old! How wonderful! And just as wonderful that I am sitting there, loving every moment of it.

Writing about my love of opera, plays, music, etc., brings back the memories of another wonderful couple: Dr. Raymond Edwards and his wife June. Raymond was the principal of the Drama School in Cardiff Castle. It was due to the efforts of Raymond that they were later moved to a new home and the College is thriving ever since. A few years ago I was approached by the BBC Radio Wales to "assess" the Sunday newspapers on the air. I must have been acceptable because a few weeks later I was offered the chance to be the 'Fashion Guru' on Jamie Owen's programme, once a week and I loved doing it. Jamie is a popular TV and radio personality and we became friends. I see him on the TV and read his beautiful books all about Wales and I even manage to talk with him on the telephone, in spite of his very tight schedule.

A few years after I moved back 'home' to Wales, I become friendly with a number of very nice people, all members of the local Lions International club. I really like the Lions because they are the only charity who does not take any money out from the donations, from the money they all (the members) work very hard for all year round. They have fundraising days, asking, begging for donations and then all the money is spent locally, every penny of it. Christmas is a special time for them, when many people, who perhaps would not receive anything, get wonderful parcels from the Lions.

I have left to last to mention a friend, no longer with us, who was very interesting, an unusual friend to have for a Jewish person. His name was Gareth Lewis and he was a clergyman. During our friendship he was made the Dean of Monmouthshire. He actually came to tell me that he had been appointed and after congratulating him I said

"I must be the only Jewish woman within a 500 mile radius who has the new Dean of an important parish, as a close friend".

My wonderful friend, Gareth said without any hesitation:

"Darling, this is what we call GLASNOST!".... (This was the time of poor great Mr. Gorbachov.

Tragically, my great friend Gareth became terribly ill, retired from the great job, moved into a beautiful flat in Cardiff, just on Cathedral Green in Llandaff. I visited him every week, cooked food he liked and food I thought he would enjoy, but even my very famous chicken soup, which has cured many friends and made them feel better didn't help him and he died. I still miss him.

As I have mentioned before, writing down all my stories was not as difficult as finding a way of finishing it. That was before the 10th April, this year when something totally unbelievable happened.

I read the Sunday Telegraph religiously while having my coffee and before 9am when my favourite programme starts on BBC Radio Wales. That is 'Golden Oldies', with the wonderful Dewi Griffiths, who is a real expert on music for us 'oldies'.

Anyway, on 10th April – it was the 60th anniversary of the liberation of the Belsen concentration camp – there was a photograph in the middle of the main part of the Telegraph, and of course I immediately recognised it as the most hellish place on earth: Bergen Belsen Concentration Camp.

The article was called 'The Gate of Hell' and there was a tiny picture on the page of a young SAS officer by the name of John Randall, then aged 24 years.

I screamed, because in front of my eyes was the face that I had been carrying around in my head for 60 years.

The article started with the words - *Lieutenant John Randall, then a 24-year-old SAS officer, was on a reconnaissance mission in northern Germany. He and his driver were heading down the road to Lüneberg when he noticed a large, imposing iron gate in front of a track leading off into the woods to their left. Curious, Randall decided to investigate, and so discovered one of the most horrifying aspects of Hitler's Germany.*

"We were totally unprepared for what we had stumbled across," says Randall, now 85, "I just drove through these gates because they were open. There were one or two totally dejected-looking German guards, but they made no effort to shoot. They didn't even stop us."

"About 30 yards into the camp, my Jeep was suddenly surrounded by a group of around 100 emaciated prisoners," recalls Randall. "Most of them were in black-and-white-striped prison uniforms and the rest wore a terrible assortment of ragged clothes. It was the state of these inmates that made me realise that this was no ordinary PoW camp. As to the identity or name of the place, I had no idea. We were two miles from Lüneberg Heath where, incidentally, Montgomery signed the German surrender." (1)

He goes on to mention that some 15 year old almost skeletons went up to him and said in various languages that they only had a few days to live and had no hope, but now that he had come, hope came back to them, etc. I was one of those 15 year olds who stood up when he entered the first barrack in the camp and tried to talk to him!

On the bottom of the page in the paper there was a bigger picture of Mr. Randall, showing him now, a very distinguished 85 year old with the SAS beret.

I sent a letter to Mr. Randall via the Daily Telegraph, and said I would love to meet him, of course.

A few days later a very gentle male voice asked if it was Mady on the phone, and I started our conversation with me shouting "Oh my God, oh my God"! I cannot believe that I am talking with the man who basically saved my life!

Mr. Randall invited me for lunch at the Special Forces Club, and it was a fantastic meeting, which happened against a billion-to-one odds. I could have been dead, could have been living in Hungary, Canada, New York, anywhere! I could have been reading any other newspaper, or even no paper, etc., etc.

If you agree with me that this is an almost unbelievable story, let me tell you about another twist in the tale that happened the week before I had my date with Mr. Randall.

I had some friends in my house, celebrating my 75th birthday actually, and Mark, son of my best friend Jane was reading the letter I had received from John Randall. Mark did not even get past the address heading on the paper, when he shouted "Mum, Mum, this is John Randall"!

Well it came out that Jane, her late husband and children were neighbours and very good friends of the Randall's' for years! Small world, eh? A very small world!

The lunch meeting was wonderful; we talked for 3 hours non-stop as easily as if we had seen each other just recently. As I said to him,

"I am very lucky because you not only turned out to be the most important man in my life, but as a bonus you are a very nice person, too!"

Interestingly the husband of a very old friend in Cardiff said: "Mady, you have now made the full circle".

John Randall said the same words during lunch. I agree with them, but there are two more little links that I need at the end of this 60 year-old chain – one is for me to meet the Randall family and for me to introduce my grandchildren to them.

Just another footnote: If there would be a world championship of huge mistakes held, I have no doubt that I would get first prize, but even I make good decisions every now and again! One of the best ones was to return to Britain after all my crazy travelling around.

Mr. Randall has also been around the world, but never to America so I could not have met him there.

Interestingly, I think everyone should read this note from my beloved hero; John Randall which he wrote following his reading of the first draft of this book.

Mady dear

I have made a few comments but I am not happy about making any more. This is your story and should remain told as "your story". It is most impressive and will appeal to lots of readers.

Prior to 1939 you lived with loving parents and relations and had the comfort of a warm and happy home and was a little girl doing well at school with a bright future. Contrast this with your war time experience of cruelty and horror – from hunger and lack of hope – but a determination to survive – deep down refusal to give in, in spite of all the odds and the sinister situation around you. The brutality of the Nazis the utter cruelty they inflicted on all who stood in their way. Your helplessness and fear – made to do anything to save yourself or the others around you.

With the war over but still no security living in an ugly world still full of hate and depravity – but still hope and determination to survive. Finally bit by bit survival and success – you have fought and have won.

Congratulations- I am proud to know you and I am lucky to have played a tiny part in your survival.

John Randall May 5th 2006

Thank you for reading my story.

THE END

Here are notes from two of my oldest and dearest friends:-

It seems incredible that fifty years have passed since I first met Mady and her three year old daughter at the refugee centre, set up by the United Nations, at Newfield Hall in Yorkshire. At that Christmas time, in 1956, I could not have foreseen that inviting them to share my home in Cardiff would have led to a friendship that has lasted so long, and during which, we seem to have become part of each others families sharing so many of life's experiences. It took no time at all for Mady to master the English language which she now so obviously loves and she has applied the same enthusiasm and energy to all of her other activities particularly into the making and keeping friends.

During the 17 years that she lived in America she always took the trouble to keep in touch with her friends. I spent a wonderful summer with her in New York and had many and varied visits to the theatre including meeting Mady's friend Victor Borge and a visit, just for my benefit, to the Yankee Stadium.

Life has not always been kind to Mady and it is quite remarkable that she has not become bitter. She is probably the most industrious and productive person I have known but it is her creative gifts that have crowned her success. Whilst she enjoyed all of the good times that her successes brought her in America her loyalty to and love of this country, especially for Wales, has remained paramount. Mady has become part of the fabric and culture of the Village where she lives and has ample opportunity to indulge in her great love of feeding and entertaining her friends.

Mady is a lover of life and I can thank her that through these long years, much of those we have shared, my life has been fuller of experiences, more colourful and adventurous than it would have otherwise been.

Dot………….. December 2006

I was never a confident person, especially at the time when I first "worked" with Mady.

During the early years with Mady, we would (whilst working, of course) discuss current affairs, films and theatre, etc., and out of this I developed as a person. In a way I have Mady to thank for having faith in me at the beginning. Left to my own devices I do not think I would have stretched myself.

I had worked as an alteration hand which I enjoyed – also in a factory which wasn't to my liking at all.

As well as being my employer we became friends.

Mady introduced me to culture, Theatre, Opera, the Arts and always invited me to join her on most social occasions.

I will always admire her courage and thank god I never had to go through what she did.

Above all we share a sense of humour, which I think is an important ingredient in a long lasting friendship, as well as a marriage

Lily………….. December 2006

Sources

Page 46 Richard Dimbleby. BBC records from Belsen, 25th April 1945.

Page 49 Law-Reports of Trials of War Criminals, The United Nations War Crimes Commission, Volume II, London, HMSO, 1947

Page 172 The gate of Hell By Alexander van Straubenzee Telegraph.co.uk Filed: 10/04/2005

Stephen, his seventeenth Birthday was on March 19th, the day the Germans invaded Hungary.

Stephanie and George, my parents, in 1929.

New York in the late 1970's. One of my "Cheesecake" photographs (the name given to these pictures in the fashion trade).

Me aged about twelve years with my aunt Elizabeth, who was an Hungarian Swimming Champion.

About 1927. Right to left seated, my mother, my maternal grandmother Francesca, my aunt Ilona. Standing right to left, my uncle Geza, my uncle Michael.

My two cousins, Ivan and Tommy, the children of my uncle Charles Glasz, he returned from a good life in Havana in the mid 1930's and married a lovely young woman named Ethel. They were all wiped out in Auschwitz.

Bergen Belsen. SS ex-guards, now prisoners, heave bodies into lorries under the supervision of British soldiers.

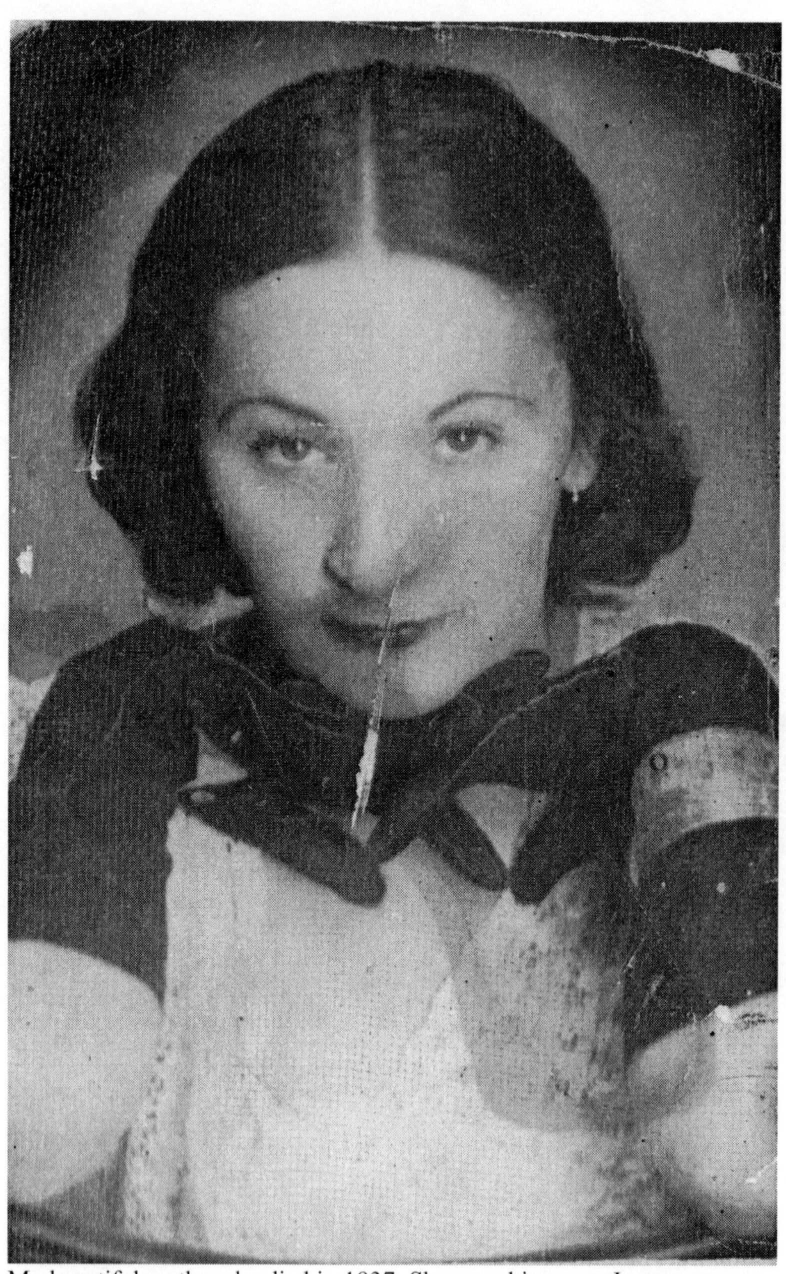

My beautiful mother she died in 1937. She was thirty one, I was seven.

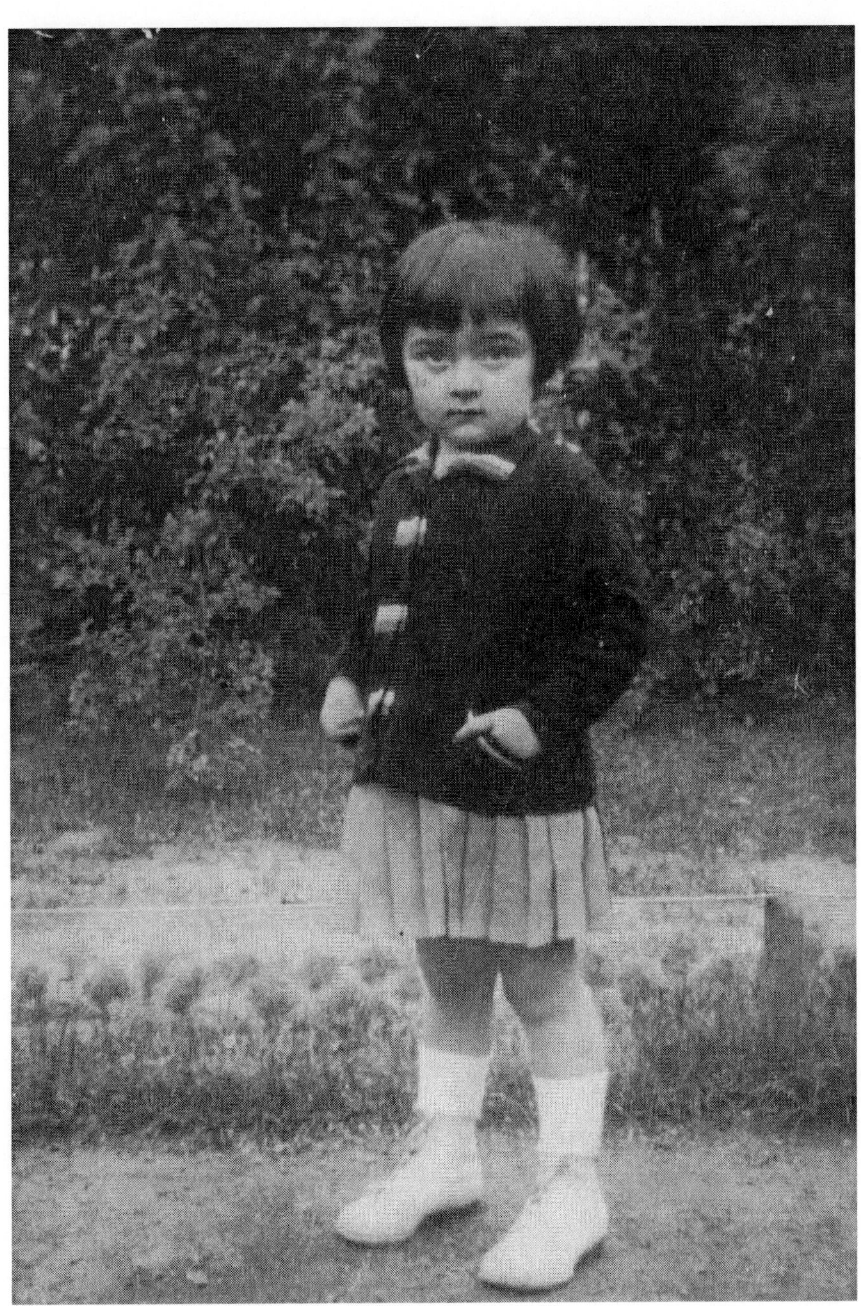

Me aged about four years.

Me aged about twelve years with George, he asked me to go out with him but I couldn't because I was going out with Stephen seriously. George became a tuberculosis specialist and died before turning 50.